PS8563.L37 Y47 1999

Glass, Joanna M

Yesteryear /

1999.

MW01121551

2007 12 03

Ye eryear

HUMBER COLLEGE
LAKESHORE CAMPUS
LEARNING RESOURCE CENTRE
3199 LAKESHORE BLVD WES

Yesteryear

JOANNA MCCLELLAND GLASS

Playwrights Canada Press
Toronto • Canada

Humber College Library

Yesteryear © Joanna McClelland Glass, 1998

Playwrights Canada Press is the publishing imprint of:
Playwrights Union of Canada
54 Wolseley Street, 2nd floor, Toronto, Ontario, M5T 1A5
Tel (416) 703-0201; Fax (416) 703-0059
E-mail: cdplays@interlog.com; Internet: www.puc.ca

CAUTION: This play is fully protected under the copyright laws of Canada and all other countries of The Copyright Union, and is subject to royalty. Changes to the script are expressly forbidden without the prior written permission of the author. Rights to produce, film, or record, in whole or in part, in any medium or any language, by any group, amateur or professional, are retained by the author. Those interested in amateur production rights are requested to apply to *Playwrights Union of Canada* (see above). Those interested in professional production rights are requested to apply to: *Barbara Hogenson Agency, 165 West End Avenue, #19C, New York, New York, 10021, Tel (212) 874-8084, Fax (212) 362-3011, E-mail bhogenson@aol.com*

No part of this book, covered by the copyright hereon, may be reproduced or used in any form or by any means—graphic, electronic or mechanical—without the prior written permission of the publisher except for excerpts in a review. Any request for photocopying, recording, taping or information storage and retrieval systems of any part of this book shall be directed to: *The Canadian Copyright Licensing Agency, 6 Adelaide Street East, Suite 900, Toronto, Ontario, M5C 1H6, Tel (416) 868-1620*

Playwrights Canada Press operates with the generous assistance of The Canada Council for the Arts—Writing and Publishing Section, and the Ontario Arts Council—Literature Office.

Canadian Cataloguing in Publication Data

Glass, Joanna M.
    Yesteryear

A play.
ISBN 0-88754-573-4

I. Title.

PS8563.L369Y47 1998   C812'.54   C99-930097-0
PR9199.3.G52Y47   1998

First edition: January 1999
Printed and bound in Canada

for Mimi Bochco

the girl from Plunge
with love and admiration

Joanna McClelland Glass' plays have been produced across North America, as well as England, Ireland, Australia, and Germany. Her one-act plays, *Canadian Gothic* and *American Modern*, were first produced in 1972 at the Manhattan Theatre Club in New York. *Artichoke* was first produced in 1974 at the Long Wharf Theatre in New Haven, Connecticut. *To Grandmother's House We Go* was first produced at the Alley Theatre in Houston, Texas, and moved to Broadway in 1980. *Play Memory* premiered at the McCarter Theatre in Princeton, N.J., and moved to Broadway in 1984, garnering a Tony nomination. *If We Are Women* premiered in 1993 at the Williamston Theatre Festival in Williamston, Mass. The 1994 Canadian premiere was a co-production between the Vancouver Playhouse and the Canadian Stage Company.

Ms. Glass has two published novels, *Reflections on a Mountain Summer* (1985) and *Woman Wanted* (1984), the latter of which was filmed as a motion picture in the summer of 1998, starring Kiefer Sutherland, Holly Hunter, and Michael Moriarity.

Production History

Yesteryear premiered in the Bluma Appel Theatre, St. Lawrence Centre, Toronto, in 1989, and was produced by the Canadian Stage Company.

The revised version was produced by Anne Chislett at the Blyth Festival, Blyth, Ontario, in the summer of 1998. That production was developed with assistance from the National Arts Centre English Theatre, Ottawa, and in co-operation with the Manitoba Theatre Centre.

Music Suggestions

Beginning of Act One: "I Can't Give You Anything But Love." Lyrics by Dorothy Fields, music by Jimmy McHugh. Mills Music Inc., 1928. Les Paul and Mary Ford recording, Capitol Records, ASCAP.

End of Act One, Scene One: "I'll Walk Alone." Lyrics by Sammy Cahn, music by Jule Styne. Morley Music Co., 1944, Cahn Music Co., 1944. From "Your Hit Parade," vocal by Frank Sinatra, Sandy Hook Records, SH 2032.

End of Act One, Scene Two: "What'll I Do?" A clarinet rendition.

Beginning of Act Two: "I'm Sending You a Big Bouquet of Roses." Vocal rendition.

End of Act Two, Scene One: "I Love You So Much, It Hurts Me." Lyrics and music by Floyd Tillman. Melody Lane Inc., 1948. Vocal by Jimmy Wakeley, ASCAP. From "Slippin' Around," Jimy Wakeley and Margaret Whiting, Capital Records, 12/18/1948.

End of Act Two, Scene Two: "Oh, Look at Me Now." Lyrics by John De Vries, music by Joe Bushkin. Embassy Music Corporation, 1941. Vocal by Maury Cross, Sammy Kaye and His Orchestra, Volume 1, Hindsight Records.

End of Act Two, Scene Three: "(The Bells Are Ringing) For Me and My Gal." Lyrics and music by George Meyer, Edgar Lesie, and E. Ray Goetz. Copyright 1917. Vocals by Judy Garland and Gene Kelly, Decca Records, 1/24/1942, ASCAP.

Note: In Act One, Scene One, the e. e. cummings poem is "Sonnet Entitled How to Run The World," from the collection *No Thanks, 1935-1938*. The quote "There is no frigate like a book, to take us lands away" is Emily Dickinson, #1263.

The Characters

DAVID McTAVISH, forty, a painter of interiors.

BETH MacMILLAN, late-thirties; pretty, prominent, lonely woman of Raglan, wife of Sandy MacMillan.

HOWARD ROBERTSON, forty, owner of Howard's Hardware.

TOM WALLACE, seventy, retired bank manager.

ANDY CAMPBELL, fifties, Police Chief of Raglan.

MALCOLM MacGREGOR, fifties, Mayor of Raglan, "larger than life."

SANDY MacMILLAN, mid-forties, husband of Beth, and owner of the Raglan Egg-Candling Plant.

BOB RAMSEY, twenty-one, telegraph and switchboard operator at the King Edward Hotel; shy and awkward, young and gawky.

EMMA DAY, in her sixties, a formidable Madam, owner of Emma Day's Whorehouse.

MILDRED DOUGLAS, thirty-five, pretty, strong-minded, optimistic; the once-intended of David McTavish.

Note: The actor playing ANDY CAMPBELL will be used, in disguise, as "Dizzy Donohue." In Act Two, Scene Three, the "Dizzy Donohue" character can be played, in disguise, by either EMMA DAY or BETH MacMILLAN. At other times the actors playing TOM WALLACE, BOB RAMSEY, MALCOLM MacGREGOR, SANDY MacMILLAN, can be used, in various disguises, as patrons in Howard's Hardware.

The Setting

The play is set in the fictional town of Raglan, Saskatchewan, in 1948. Raglan is a small prairie city of fifty thousand. It is summertime, late in the day, a Tuesday.

The curtain rises on a large room that is the "back room" of Howard's Hardware. In the back wall there is an opened door, leading to the hardware store proper. The back wall is mostly shelving that houses stock of hardware—twine, washboards, bins of nails, tools, paint cans. One of the shelves is reserved for the glasses and whisky bottles that belong to the men who come to visit DAVID and HOWARD. There may be pails and buckets hanging from the ceiling, stacked spades, rakes, hoes, pitchforks, brooms, etc. Possibly there is a woodstove. There is also a door, stage right, that leads to a back alley. One must either enter there, or through the hardware store proper.

We must be able to see, through a portion of the back wall, a portion of the actual store—possibly no more than an old counter and a cash register. There may be a front-door bell that signals the coming and going of HOWARD's customers.

This back room is HOWARD's storage room, but it also serves as DAVID McTAVISH's home. In the "social" area, there are three or four wooden chairs, and a wide "deacon" type of bench. This bench also functions as a trundle bed, which is where DAVID sleeps. In "DAVID's domain" there is a large, very visible framed photograph of EMMA DAY's Victorian house. There is a small table with one chair, a length of pipe on which his few clothes hang, a small bureau, and a bookcase. Also, behind a curtain, there is a sink and a toilet. There is a small cabinet that has a hot plate on it, and an ice-box. Nearby is a shelf containing his meager collection of dishes and pots. The general impression is one of austerity.

DAVID McTAVISH, a bachelor, is Raglan's leading painter of interiors. As the play begins, he is wearing paint-spattered white denim overalls with a cotton shirt. He is in the middle of an argument with BETH MacMILLAN, who is attractive and well dressed. When HOWARD enters, he wears a denim apron over his trousers and shirt.

Act One, Scene One

As the curtain rises, the "back room" is empty. DAVID's trundle bed is open and messy.

In the hardware store proper, we vaguely see HOWARD ROBERTSON with a customer (BOB RAMSEY in disguise). Separately, we see BETH MacMILLAN and DAVID McTAVISH in an argument. We hear loud voices.

DAVID   *(heatedly)* How on earth can you say that?

BETH   I can say it very easily! I can say it with no effort at all!

DAVID guides BETH out of the store, into the back room.

DAVID   *(adamantly)* In here please, if you don't mind.

BETH   *What* is the matter?

DAVID   I don't wish to conduct this business in front of Howard's customers. *(brief pause)* Sorry, I haven't had a chance to make my bed. *(going to it)* It's a trundle.

BETH   A trundle? David McTavish, I have to say that a trundle bed, at your age, is a very sad thing.

He quickly makes the bed and slides it under the bench.

DAVID   Yes, well, better a trundle than a marriage bed that's hell on earth.

BETH	What would you know about marriage beds?
DAVID	*(attempting composure)* Mrs. MacMillan, I'm a man who's slow to anger. I've spent the last fifteen years of my life avoiding anger. But there was, in what you said in the store, an inference that's got my ire up.
BETH	Inference? There was no inference. An inference is when something's inferred. When I say you're out to cheat the MacMillans, I don't infer. Last week you gave me an estimate for one coat of paint—oil base—and today you went to my house and had a look at it, and now you tell me the job'll take two coats oil base. At twice the price, naturally. A week ago I went home to Sandy and I said, "It's all set. McTavish'll do it for a reasonable price." Today your price is doubled and it's no longer reasonable. I am saying, in plain King's English, you're trying to cheat the MacMillans.
DAVID	Mrs. MacMillan, you're being very harsh.
BETH	I suppose, if I returned next week to these strangely appointed digs you call your home, you'd tell me, "Oh, there was an error. The estimate didn't include the woodwork, as you thought. It'll be thirty dollars more for the window frames and the doors!"
DAVID	Mrs. MacMillan, an estimate is an *estimation*.
BETH	David, you're aware that mine is a large house.
DAVID	I am. It's the third largest house in Raglan.
BETH	The second largest, second only to the house of the Mayor.
DAVID	The third largest. The largest house in Raglan is Emma Day's whorehouse.

BETH	Well, yes, Emma Day's is quite grand. But it isn't in town, is it? It's on the outskirts, which is entirely fitting considering the sort of disreputable place it is. If you insist on doubling your price, I'll simply have to hire McGinty.
DAVID	Mrs. MacMillan, McGinty paints barns. Barn painters work in the open. They're notoriously sloppy, with no regard for fine furniture. You wouldn't want McGinty wielding a brush in your house.
BETH	The word on the vine, David, is that McGinty'd give his eye teeth to do an interior. That he'd do one *gratis*, just to "get his foot in the door," so to speak.
DAVID	Mrs. MacMillan, I have a fine established reputation. As my little ad in the paper says: "David McTavish—no muss, no fuss." McGinty is known far and wide as a dripper.
BETH	Oh, you're such an obstinate man! You've turned into an obstinate, spinster of a man!

DAVID *marches to the back-alley door.*

BETH	What do you think you're doing?
DAVID	I am showing you the door before I overspeak myself.
BETH	How dare you!
HOWARD	*(hollering from the hardware)* Everything all right back there, Davey?
DAVID	*(hollering)* Hunky dory, Howard. Don't bother yourself.

Another CUSTOMER *enters the hardware; it is* SANDY MacMILLAN *in disguise.*

BETH	Sir, as the good Lord said in the olive grove, "An eye for an eye." You'll have Sandy MacMillan at your door this evening, and you will apologize for this insult!
DAVID	*(angrily)* I will not have Sandy at my door this evening! This is Tuesday, and Sandy's visited Emma Day's whorehouse every Tuesday for a full decade. He goes on Tuesday and he engages the services of Lizzie Evans. You know it, and I know it, and all your kith and kin know it!

> BETH *is deeply wounded. She becomes weepy.*

BETH	Those comments, sir, are harsh.
DAVID	Oh, God, I'm sorry! I apologize. I went too far. *(flustered)* Please, come and sit down.
BETH	I know it's on the lips of half the town. The brass of the town, especially, have made my predicament their favorite gossip. They call him "Randy Sandy," don't they? But I didn't expect you, David, not being part of the brass of the town—
DAVID	Not being part of the brass, I forgot my place. I forgot that I'm a simple laborer, and Sandy MacMillan owns the egg-candling plant. But you called me a cheat and it rankled me out of control. There's only one thing I'm ashamed of in a life span of forty years, and that's—well—
BETH	The nasty business with Mildred Douglas.
DAVID	Yes.
BETH	David, as scandals go, that one rated four stars. My goodness, you were an explosive young man. In fact, you were called "Mr. Volcano" in our high-school yearbook.
DAVID	And you, quite rightly, were called "the most likely to succeed."

BETH	*(pointedly staring at the hotplate)* Is that a teapot I see by your hotplate?
DAVID	It is.
BETH	Does it have any brew in it now?
DAVID	It does. I made it fresh as you arrived.
BETH	*(wearily)* I find that as I myself approach forty, I have less and less stomach for arguments. I could use a spot of tea.

Suddenly DAVID *shouts, behind him:*

DAVID	Howard? Mrs. MacMillan's asking for a spot of tea. Can you join us?
HOWARD	*(hollering)* Not now, Davey, thank you.
DAVID	*(finding a cup)* Howard's got a new load of screwdrivers in today. *(contritely)* Beth, I shouldn't have thrown Emma Day in your face like that.
BETH	Years ago, you always called me Beth.
DAVID	Years ago we were in high school. Your social status is much more clearly defined in 1948.
BETH	Actually, David, it wasn't the mention of Emma Day that hurt me. It was the mention of kith and kin. If I had kith, I'd more easily bear the disgrace of it all.
DAVID	*(giving her the tea)* I'm sorry you haven't.
BETH	It wasn't meant to be. But it does make my days a little hollow. I live under a terrible strain, David. No babies by my hearth, and a philandering husband. Perhaps I overreacted to your second estimate.

DAVID   Here's the crux of it. You didn't tell me you had cabbage-rose wallpaper. Cabbage roses are bloody miserable things to hide. If you insist on one coat, I'll have to remove the paper. That'll quadruple your price in labor. Two coats oil base doubles my quote, covers the roses, but cuts your ultimate cost by half.

BETH   I see. Yes.

DAVID   You were somewhat remiss in not mentioning the roses.

BETH   I was. I'm afraid, since I married Sandy, the practicalities of life never occur to me.

DAVID   Beth, you are a walking practicality. And that, quite frankly, is a mystery to the town, because you left our old neighborhood and married up to the egg-candling plant. And yet you penny-pinch, and you haggle—

BETH   I get it from my dad. My dad came to this prairie nearly barefoot from Glasgow. When I was just a wee slip of a lass, my dad said *(with a Scottish accent)* "Beth, here's a nickel. You can take it and buy a bag of Planter's Peanuts. But remember this: If you don't buy the peanuts, and you save nickels 'till you have twenty, you'll have a dollar."

DAVID   I don't recall your dad ever haggling.

Another customer, ANDY CAMPBELL *as "Dizzy Donohue," enters the store.*

BETH   More's the pity. What he preached at home he didn't practice at his smithy. Does everyone call me a haggler?

DAVID   Well, you're known to be difficult where money's concerned.

BETH
And you're known to be the gloomiest man in town! Sandy calls you a "sad sack." Why have you let that old scandal sit so heavy on your soul?

DAVID
Let's just say that I'm carrying a torch.

BETH
But you live here like a hermit, in the back of Howard's Hardware. You could afford some creature comforts, but all I see here is a hotplate, a few meager dishes, and—Heavens—a trundle bed. And Sandy says that even when you're gathered with the men, you sneak off into a corner and read your poems. Sandy doesn't know why you bother to gather at all.

DAVID
I don't gather. The men gather because Howard's Hardware's on the Main Street, and they all keep bottles here in Howard's back room. Your Sandy has a lot of crust, passing judgment on other people. Did you know, your Sandy thinks that up in Heaven everyone has an occupation?

BETH
Does he?

DAVID
He thinks the general populace are tradesmen, but it's God who runs the egg-candling plant.

They have a small chuckle.

BETH
Isn't this nice? Tea for two, and a little laugh.

HOWARD *enters, hurriedly.*

HOWARD
(looking for a small box) S'cuse me. I've got an exchange.

DAVID
Dizzy Donohue?

HOWARD
Uh huh. He bought a three-eighth's wrench when he needed a nine-sixteen. S'cuse me.

HOWARD *leaves.*

BETH
David, do you ever paint at Emma Day's?

DAVID   Every two years. It's a beautiful old house.
                   (pointing) I've tacked up a picture of it, over there.

BETH   Just how many—women—work there?

DAVID   Four or five, I think.

BETH   And Lizzie Evans, what does she look like?

DAVID   Well, gee. She looks like a tart.

BETH   Good. I'm glad. David, years ago—do you
                   remember?—you kissed me once on a Halloween
                   hayride.

DAVID   *(hollering)* Howard? You're sure you can't join us
                   for a spot of tea?

HOWARD   *(hollering)* Not now, Davey. Busy out here.

DAVID   He's got a special load of screwdrivers in today.
                   Sheffield steel. Good solid man, Howard.

BETH   It's a shame he's never married. He lives with his
                   maiden sister, doesn't he?

DAVID   Yes. Jane. She's joined the Salvation Army.

BETH   That kiss is indelible in my memory, because it
                   wasn't a simple lip-kiss. It was my introduction—
                   my baptism, one might say—to the French kiss. I
                   liked you very much, David, but in those days you
                   had nothing to your name but a ladder and brush.
                   And then you went off to the RCAF, and flew that
                   Spitfire in the war.

DAVID   I never flew a Spitfire. I don't know how that
                   rumor got started.

BETH   I thought you were so handsome in your uniform.
                   And when you came back, I thanked God for saving
                   you from the Krauts. And I was thankful that you
                   didn't bring home a war bride.

DAVID	I went to war. I didn't go courting.
BETH	But now you're successful. You've got at least a hundred regular customers, and the Mayor contracts you to paint the Library. Mildred Douglas would kick herself around the block if she knew how well you were doing.
DAVID	No, she wouldn't.
	Both customers now leave the hardware store.
BETH	Millie and I were the prettiest girls in town, but I knew what I wanted. Millie never did manage to get her ducks in a row.
DAVID	Beth, all the world's a marketplace. You put your looks on the marriage market. Millie put hers on what you might call the free market, and they say in the town she had hard times after she left Raglan. It's certain she doesn't have silver from Birks and a Queen Anne highboy, as you do.
	HOWARD *enters, gets a carton, and quickly leaves.*
DAVID	Howard, you'll get the hernia from those cartons. Come take a break.
HOWARD	Not now, David, thank you. *(to BETH)* Screwdrivers
BETH	Yes.
HOWARD	Phillips.
BETH	Ah.
HOWARD	Sheffield steel. *(to DAVID)* Have you concluded your business?
DAVID	Very nearly.

HOWARD	Good. We're expecting the gents.

HOWARD *exits.*

BETH	I must go. I've a man coming to measure new draperies. Can you begin tomorrow?
DAVID	I'll be there at eight a.m., and I can promise you a honey of a job.

BETH *sighs deeply, as she gathers to go.*

BETH	Oh, David, isn't life a puzzle?
DAVID	It is.
BETH	I sometimes pause and reflect on it. Not frequently, of course, because it nearly always causes migraine. You and I must have thought our youthful behavior was justified. Your hot temper, for instance. When you were eighteen, and your mum died, and there wasn't money for a coffin, you went to the funeral home and punched out the undertaker. Rumor had him requiring ten stitches. And, again, when you found Millie with the goalie and you went berserk. You behaved that way because you were convinced that justice must be sought, and hang the consequences. And I, well, do you know why I set my cap for Sandy MacMillan?
DAVID	I do.
BETH	I've never told this to a soul. In Grade Twelve all the girls had new dresses for graduation. My smithy of a dad hadn't a penny, and you know what my mum did? She bought an old parachute at an Air Force surplus sale. She treadled away for two whole days on her Singer, and I wore that piece of white sleaze to the ceremony. I took my diploma in hand, and as I walked back to my seat I whispered to myself, "Sandy MacMillan's the only way out of this." *(brief pause)* I'll look for you at eight in the morning.

DAVID   I'll be there. But when I paint, I paint. I don't drink tea.

BETH   Oh, David, you've really become a curmudgeon!

                 BETH *moves quickly through the Hardware and out the front door.*

BETH   Goodbye, Howard!

HOWARD   Goodbye, Mrs. MacMillan.

                 HOWARD *runs into the back room.* DAVID *begins setting up for the expected men.*

HOWARD   Sweet Petunia! What was that all about?

DAVID   Cabbage roses! Howard, you know what's wrong with that woman?

HOWARD   What?

DAVID   She didn't get enough Planter's Peanuts in her youth.

                 DAVID *laughs.* HOWARD *looks dimwitted.*

HOWARD   Planter's Peanuts?

DAVID   *(looking at his watch)* Six o'clock, Howard. Best turn off your lights.

HOWARD   *(heading into the Hardware)* Didja notice that the Daffodil Yellow came in, for the library?

DAVID   I can't paint the library this fiscal year.

HOWARD   Sez who?

DAVID   Sez Hizzonor the Mayor.

                 DAVID *continues to set up seating.*

HOWARD	I thought the Council contracted for it.
DAVID	They did, but there's no money left in the till.
HOWARD	*(angrily)* I can't believe this pack of donkeys we've got on the Council!
DAVID	Now, now, Howard, mustn't be too harsh.

> HOWARD *fills a pitcher of water at* DAVID*'s sink and places it near the bottles and glasses.*

HOWARD	They let the Raglan library go to seed, while they're throwing out perfectly good trolleys for modern buses. I have to say, Davey, it galls me that you take it all so lightly.
DAVID	I don't take it lightly, I take it silently. Howard, when I was young I had crystal clear convictions. There was right and there was wrong, and I didn't— as the song says—I didn't mess with Mister-in-Between. I let my opinions be known at the Barber Shop, the Pool Hall, City Hall, and they called me a hot-head and a lunatic.
HOWARD	They called you, in fact, "Maniac McTavish." Some said you were actually certifiable. I'm glad you no longer rant and rave but, in my opinion, you've mellowed yourself into mush.
DAVID	No, I haven't. I've had to learn that there's right and wrong, and "in-between" is where most people live. Mildred Douglas seemed to know that at birth. We both lived in cramped little hovels, we both saw how crippling poverty was, but Mildred didn't explode in rage. She went and taught an Indian kid to read. She went and read to the blind.
HOWARD	Well, you botched that one up royally.
DAVID	*I* botched it up??

HOWARD   You didn't even seek an explanation! You loved her one day, then you found her in flagrunt with—

DAVID   Found her what?

HOWARD   The Latin term—in flagrunt with the goalie, and you ran her out of town. And when you did that, Sally Ballintine at the hairdresser's called the mental asylum in Weyburn and asked them to come commit you. *(heatedly)* David, I met Millie in a sandbox when she was two years old. When you ran her out of town, I lost the best friend I ever had. *(there is a knock at the back door)* Ah, well, here comes the banker.

                           TOM WALLACE *bustles in. He is seventy, nattily dressed, the ex-manager of the Bank of Raglan.*

TOM   Hello, David. Hello, Howard. Six o'clock, lads.

DAVID &
HOWARD   Hello, Tom. Good to see you.

TOM   *(getting his bottle and drink)* Never retire, lads, never retire. Stay in harness as long as you can. Nothin' to do the whole damn day but drink tea with the better-half and listen to her prattle. When I was manager of the bank, I was well versed in first mortgages, second mortgages, interest rates, collateral, and when all else failed, the legal intricacies of filin' for bankruptcy. I knew every piece of property in Raglan and all the appurtenances thereon. Now my brain cells are dead and my stomach's lined with tanic acid. It's my instinct for survival that gets me here at six. Finished early today, did you, David?

DAVID   I didn't work the whole day long. I had a misunderstanding with a client.

HOWARD   Beth MacMillan.

During the following, DAVID *and* HOWARD *get their drinks.*

TOM   Ah ha! Well, I've a piece of gossip in that regard. Did you know that Sandy MacMillan is now deprived of butter at his table? Too expensive. She cuts corners, I'm told, by buyin' this new oleomargarine stuff. She spends an hour every day kneading her margarine.

HOWARD   Needing her marg—?

TOM   *(illustrating) Kneading*, Howard, with a "k." The way they do bread. Apparently this margarine comes white, in a plastic pouch. Looks like lard. And there's a little sort of pellet in it, filled with yellow coloring. You give it a punch to burst the pellet and then you knead it with your knuckles— that's knuckles, Howard, with a "k"—for an hour, 'till it's soft and the color spreads through. And by doin' all that, Beth MacMillan saves Sandy approximately twenty-five cents a week.

HOWARD   Creepin' Ivy! *(his expletive)*

There's another knock at the door.

DAVID   That'll be the copper.

ANDY CAMPBELL bursts in, in uniform. He is Raglan's Police Chief.

ANDY   Hello, lads, time to wet the whistle. My God, what a day! You lads think this town is all milk and honey. Picnics and hayrides, Saskatoon berries in August, apple cider in September, plum pudding at Christmas. *(going to the bottle shelf)* Today I stopped a suicide off the Railroad Bridge.

TOM   Dear me, a suicide?

HOWARD   Now, Andy, you know that Crown Royal belongs to the Mayor.

ANDY	Oh, for heaven's sake it does, it does. My mistake.
HOWARD	I believe yours is the Hiram Walker.
ANDY	It is, it is. My eyesight's failin'. Have to get the bi-focals soon. There she was, a teenage lass whose father works at the Wheat Pool. She'd got herself impregnated and didn't know where to turn. *(he waits for a response)* Her father's a manager at the Wheat Pool, a recent widower, and known to you all. And as I'm draggin' her to safe port, she says, "Oh, sir, I'm at your mercy and I need information."
HOWARD	What kind of information?
ANDY	Where to get an abortion.
HOWARD	Jumpin' Juniper !
DAVID	Dear God—
ANDY	Yes. Well, I knew that'd offend the sensibilities of Tweedledee and Tweedledum. You two are interchangeable, with one notable exception. David still curses occasionally—but you, Howard, since your sister joined the Salvation Army, all you can say is "Sweet Petunia," "Creepin' Ivy," "Jumpin' Juniper." *(in frustration)* It irritates the hell out of me when a man can't conjure up a good curse. Now, what were we on about?
TOM	The widower's daughter. I daresay, if she lined your pockets you'd put her onto the right party.
ANDY	Thomas, I don't like your inference.
HOWARD	Andy, this here where we are ain't your leather-upholstered office. It's the back of my Hardware. This is where we air our terrible truths and put them to bed with a bit of John Barleycorn. Your palms are greasy, Andy, and the proof of it lies in the continued operation of that whorehouse on the outskirts.

ANDY
Lads, I'm proud to have Emma Day in this town. She's an old socialist, y'know, red in her youth, gettin' pinker as she ages. You could even go so far as to say that Emma Day practices commerce with a conscience. She's a champion of the local underdog, she runs an orderly house, she don't disturb the peace, and her taxes add a large amount to Hizzoner's coffers.

HOWARD
Still, it's known that Emma Day went to Yaeger's Furs and bought a mink stole. And that stole was next seen bein' worn on the shoulders of *your* better-half!

ANDY
Hang on, now. *(he sniffs the air, loudly)* Something's missing today. Conspicuous in its absence. I don't smell the turpentine. *(to* DAVID*)* How come you're not cleaning brushes?

DAVID
Didn't work today.

TOM
Had a nasty run-in with a woman known to us all.

HOWARD
Beth MacMillan.

ANDY
Let me tell you a terrible truth about the MacMillans. Didja ever wonder what they do with all their loot? Are they investin' in Canada bonds? Are they fiscally loyal to their native soil? No, sir. They're investing in meat-packin' plants in Chicago. They're fiscal traitors. What we need, Atlantic to Pacific, is an electric fence along the 49th parallel.

DAVID
(very frustrated) And here it comes again!

ANDY
What?

DAVID
The favorite Canadian pastime. Yelpin' about our superiority to the Yanks. Wonderin' why they fail to get the message.

HOWARD   Andy, it's all in the numbers. We don't have enough people up here. We've got the biggest land mass next to Russia, but we haven't got enough of our own investors.

ANDY   And the ones we've got are Presbyterian down to their pockets. I'm one myself, so I shouldn't say it, but if there's one damn thing "Pissbyterians" can't abide, it's risk.

TOM   I've never begrudged the Yanks their money. What galls me about our great, fat neighbor is they're sayin' *they* won the war. The US of A is triumphant! Where were they in '39? Where were they all through '40, when we had whole battalions bein' butchered? They were sitting on their bums while we held the Hun at bay. Why don't you ever speak to this, David? You were in there in the thick of it, piloting that Spitfire.

DAVID   I never flew a Spitfire. Thomas, we needed their men, their money, and their munitions. And it was bloody carnage for us all. Why speak to who got in when? Why don't we ever speak to the defeat we'd have suffered if they'd never come in at all?

ANDY   McTavish, I can't believe you've become so effin' rational. I can't believe, lads, that this is the same man who caught Mildred Douglas kissin' a goalie in the backseat of a car—

DAVID *goes to his table and books.*

TOM   Andrew, it *was* the night before their wedding.

ANDY   And his brain exploded, and he took a horse-whip in hand and chased her through the town, screamin' bloody murder.

> *There is a loud knock at the back door.*
> MALCOLM MacGREGOR, *the Mayor,*
> *enters and fills the room. The first thing we*
> *notice is his out-stretched arm, bent slightly*
> *in a hand-shaking position.* MALCOLM'*s*
> *arm is ever-ready throughout the play. He*
> *"works" the room:*

MALCOLM Good evening, lads! Thomas, good to see you. How's your hammer hangin'?

TOM Feebly, Malcolm, feebly.

MALCOLM Howard, I saw your sister Jane in front of Neilson's Department Store, bangin' on her drum. Admirable. Absolutely admirable, standin' there like a stoic in the noonday sun, bangin' on her drum. Andrew, lad, I was sayin' today to a foreign fella out at the university that we Canadians believe in peace, order, and good government. I said that here in Raglan peace and order fall to you in the Police Department, and good government falls to me. Mayor of Raglan. Monarch of all I survey. *(near* DAVID'*s book stack)* David, I see you've made another trip to the library.

DAVID I go once a week to refuel.

MALCOLM Be a good lad and pour me a drink. Are you still doing battle with the librarian?

DAVID *(getting the drink)* I am.

ANDY Miss Logan's a cantankerous old biddy.

DAVID No, she isn't. She has a catholic knowledge.

ANDY Really? I didn't know.

DAVID Andy, in this case that doesn't mean Roman. Webster's says "catholic" also means *comprehensive*. Miss Logan and I just happen to have a running argument over what's a poem and what isn't.

TOM	Well, I know what a poem is: "My heart's in the highlands, my heart is not here. My heart's in the highlands a-chasing the deer."
MALCOLM	That is a poem. Easy to get consensus on that. We Scots gave the world four great things: whiskey, golf, curling, and Robbie Burns. What, in Miss Logan's estimation, is a poem?
DAVID	*(getting a book)* She made me bring this home. She said it would "broaden my horizons." Get a load of this, now: *(reading)* "A always don't there B being no such thing for C can't casts no shadow D drink and E eat of her voice in whose silence—" Well, it goes on in that vein.
HOWARD	Leapin' Lilacs!
ANDY	Does it go on in that vein through the whole damn alphabet?
TOM	I don't get the gist of it—
MALCOLM	What the hell's it trying to say?
DAVID	It's written by somebody called e. e. cummings. Two initials, no capital letters.
ANDY	Bloody drivel is what it is. Here's what I'd do, Malcolm. I'd tell old Logan if she spends tax-payer money on one more volume of drivel like that, the library won't get painted this fiscal year.
HOWARD	The library *don't* get painted this fiscal year. Malcolm made the commitment, then Malcolm reneged, because Malcolm's in a public transportation competition with Winnipeg, or some similar metropolis.
MALCOLM	Oh, Howard, please. I come here at twilight for a gab and a relax—I don't come here for recriminations. The old trams were obsolete. The new buses are expensive. The needs of the town are infinite. The budget is finite.

HOWARD	And isn't it fun, ordering buses? You and the Council have spent six months rolling little model buses around your executive table like giddy boys in a toy store.
DAVID	The truth of the matter is that buses take precedence over books. Now, this I will speak to. Malcolm, buses are only machinery. They're built to be obsolete in five years and they stink up the air with their fuel exhaust. I can go down to the library and read Chaucer's observations from Canterbury six-hundred years ago. It seems to me that knowledge should have a priority over machinery. There's no damned posterity in buses.
MALCOLM	David, you may be a master painter, but you fail to understand political reality. The travelling public is large. The reading public is small. More voters travel than read.
	There is a loud pounding on the back door. BOB RAMSEY *hurries in. He is the twenty-one-year-old switchboard and telegraph operator at the King Edward Hotel. He carries a telegram.*
BOB	Oh, Mr. McTavish! Holy Moley, I'm glad you're here. I ran down from the hotel thinkin' "What if he isn't there? What if he's somewhere else? What if he's someplace I can't find him?"
MALCOLM	*(with arm out)* I don't believe I've had the pleasure.
BOB	Oh, my God, you're the Mayor. I've never met you and I never thought I would.
MALCOLM	Give me your name, lad, and I'll never forget it.
BOB	I'm Robert Ramsey, sir. I run the switchboard and telegraph at the King Edward Hotel.
ANDY	Is there trouble at the hotel?

BOB   No, sir, I was just sittin' there, at the telegraph, and everything was normal. Mr. Chisholm was across the hall, makin' out pay cheques for the chambermaids. *(to HOWARD)* Your sister Jane came in, wearing her little blue bonnet, and went into the lounge. She was tired, y'know, from luggin' her big drum up from Neilson's Department Store, and she ordered a pot of tea. A salesman from the Swift Meat Company was complaining at the desk, sayin' his bed was too soft for his back, and he needed a board under the mattress. He was sayin' if he didn't get the board he'd want the King Eddie Hotel to provide a chiropractor. And then this came across the wire for Mr. McTavish. Oh, Mr. McTavish, it's the most incredible thing. *(he gives the cable to DAVID)* You've won the Irish Sweepstakes!

DAVID   What?

HOWARD   Holy Hollyhocks!

TOM   The Irish Sweepstakes?

ANDY   What a piece of news!

MALCOLM   Hallelujah!

BOB   Open it, sir, open it!

DAVID   *(stunned)* This must be a prank.

BOB   It's a hundred and twenty thousand dollars. Read it!

DAVID   *(dazed)* It's true. One hundred and twenty thousand, tax free.

TOM   Wait until this hits the streets!

ANDY   This absolutely cooks the goose!

             HOWARD *jumps up on a box and sings. They all join in, amidst handshakes, dances, ad libs.*

ALL	"For he's a jolly good fellow, for he's a jolly good fellow, for he's a jolly good fellow, that nobody can deny."
DAVID	Thank you, thank you, thank you. Oh, Lord, when I saw the cable I thought my old Aunt Ruth in Halifax was wirin' me that she'd died. I can't absorb it. I mean, what's it going to mean? Bobby, I'm giving you a slug of the Mayor's Crown Royal. In fact, we'll *all* have a nip of Hizzoner's Crown Royal.
MALCOLM	Will you now?
DAVID	I'll replace it with a full case tomorrow.
	He makes the rounds, filling the glasses. The back door flies open, and SANDY MacMILLAN *enters. His clothing is rumpled, his tie askew; he has been drinking at* EMMA DAY*'s whorehouse.*
SANDY	Land o' Goshen! Is it true what I've heard?
TOM	Well, it's Randy Sandy—and on a Tuesday night!
SANDY	Direct from the whorehouse. Is it true it's one hundred and twenty thousand smackeroos?
DAVID	I can't believe it's not a prank.
SANDY	Oh, it's no prank. I heard it announced on Emma Day's radio. Who sold you the ticket?
DAVID	Actually, it was your Lizzie, Sandy—at the whorehouse.
SANDY	Well, ain't that just my bum luck. David, pour me a—sorry—s'cuse me—Howard, pour me a drink, will you, lad?
HOWARD	*(doing so)* You've had a bellyful already.

SANDY   Feeling no pain, lads, feeling no pain. Except, of course, the pain that never subsides. The pain that don't ebb, don't ever wane, the daily, domestic, conjugal pain. It's worse than gangrene. *(taking the drink)* Well, Sufferin' Succotash. This, what's happened, is an Act of God. Who in Raglan is more deserving of a windfall? What a saga, David! Your hopes were dashed when Mildred Douglas betrayed you—

BOB   Who?

SANDY   What?

BOB   Who is Mildred Douglas?

SANDY   What's this snot-nosed kid doin' here?

DAVID   This is Bob Ramsey, Sandy, from the telegraph at the King Eddie.

SANDY   Well, give him a tip and send him home.

DAVID   Bobby, Mildred Douglas is a woman I loved in my youth. I was very harsh then, very judgmental.

SANDY   Mildred Douglas had carnal knowledge with a goalie, and David chased her through town with a horse-whip in hand.

BOB   My, my, my. *(he downs his drink)*

DAVID   *(a little drunk)* And I called her—to my eternal shame—a tramp and a hussy.

BOB   *(to DAVID)* May I help m'self?

DAVID   Certainly.

BOB   *(pouring another drink)* Mr. McTavish, I've no right to opinions, bein' a snot-nosed kid, but I'd venture to say that this is, potentially, a very sad story.

SANDY	The goalie swooped down, like Nelson Eddy with the whole effin' RCMP, rescued her, and took her to Toronto.
HOWARD	Now, Bobby, this is gossip. My sister Jane says gossip is the work of the devil. But I have to say that this goalie—Cammy Sinclair—had sexual congress with a whole legion of local girls.
ANDY	Like who?
HOWARD	Not for me to—
ANDY	Yeah, yeah, yeah. Who?
HOWARD	Not for me to ruin the reputations of what are now Raglan's matrons.
BOB	Oh, Mr. McTavish, this is thick. How did you ever recover?
SANDY	He went off to the war and flew a Spitfire. And what a miserable little life he's led since, in this wretched back room, doin' menial labour. Goin' from house to house, wall to wall, square foot by square foot. But these winnings are proof of what the good Lord said at Gethsemane. "The meek shall inherit the earth."
BOB	Sir, I don't think that was Gethsemane.
SANDY	It damn well was.
BOB	Don't think so.
SANDY	Then where was it?
ANDY	Musta bin Nazareth.
BOB	Don't think so.
MALCOLM	How 'bout Jericho?

BOB	Sirs, safest thing to say, when you don't know, is "The Holy Land." *(very tipsy)* Mr. McTavish, I'll bet Vera Lynn had you and Miss Douglas in mind when she sang: *(singing)* "We'll meet again, don't know where, don't know when—"
SANDY	Kid, can it.
BOB	*(singing)* "But I know we'll meet again some sunny day."
SANDY	David, I think we can call this, after all your trials and tribulations, divine intervention. It's the first time anybody's ever won anything in Raglan.
TOM	No, no, remember the Gordon brothers? There were four brothers, all magnificent curlers, and they won four Buicks at the Bonspiel.
BOB	Speech, Mr. McTavish, speech!
DAVID	Oh, I never could. And I mustn't drink too much or I won't make it to your mansion, Sandy, in the morning.
SANDY	You don't mean, with this change of fortune, you're gonna go slap paint on my walls?
DAVID	I must. I have my word. But, God, it's comin' over me like a revelation. *(suddenly ecstatic)* I don't have to, do I?
ANDY	Lad, you could go on a spree, spend half of these winnings, and still never work another day. You can sleep until noon—
TOM	You can buy your own ship and travel the world. God, I've always wanted to go to Burma.
DAVID	Oh, I don't want to travel. I've had my fill of foreign lands. And as that Yankee lady wrote, "There is no frigate like a book, to take us lands away."

ANDY	David, I'd like to retract what I said before about Tweedledee and Tweedledum. Howard, you get retracted in the bargain.
HOWARD	Thank you. Bobby, Heavens, you've had two snorts and you're empty again.
TOM	A little caution, laddie. It ain't Coca-Cola.
MALCOLM	Robert Ramsey, it's Seagram's Crown Royal. It's meant to be savoured, not guzzled. *(beginning a "campaign")* David, right here tonight, in the town of Raglan, we've got the stuff dreams are made of. What'll you splurge on first?
DAVID	Well, I'll keep my old truck, but I might buy a car. For Sundays.
MALCOLM	I'd like to make a prediction. I have some acumen in this regard, because I know *people.* Call it insight, instinct, intuition—whatever it is, it came to me with mother's milk. Give me five minutes with a man and I've got him pegged. I know what his income is, how much he's got in the bank. I know where he buys his clothes and what he spends on 'em. When he opens his mouth, I know where his ancestors came from. I predict, David, that you'll want to do something for the people of Raglan.
DAVID	Oh, I'd like that, but it's too soon to know. I thought I'd spend the rest of my life painting walls and missing Mildred Douglas
BOB	*(singing again)* "Keep smiling through, just like you always do—"
SANDY	The kid's pissed.
MALCOLM	David, let's address the keen interest you have in the library. The place is falling apart at the seams and wants the wrecker's ball. What would you

	think of a lovely new structure, with a plaque on the corner callin' it the "David McTavish Memorial Library"?
DAVID	I wouldn't want the plaque on the corner.
SANDY	David, let's you and me discuss *investments*.
DAVID	Sandy, your kind of investments wouldn't benefit the town. I'd want, somehow, to enhance the town.
BOB	Conventions.
SANDY	What say?
BOB	Mr. Chisholm, at the King Eddie, says Raglan needs to attract conventions.
ANDY	Nonsense! Masses of men, away from home, are disgusting. They can't hold their liquor, they wander the streets at two in the morning and piss on your snapdragons.
TOM	If I were you, David, I'd build a great, stone fountain in the middle of town. With water spurting out in pretty patterns, and benches all around for people to sit on.
HOWARD	Davey, you should talk to my sister Jane—
MALCOLM	*(a little tipsy)* Admirable woman, Jane, bangin' on her drum in the noonday sun.
HOWARD	*(drunkenly quoting his sister)* Jane's got a tendency to harp on this string. She says we've got a sociological debt to the Indians. She says this debt diminishes all of us— *(holding up his fingers, one by one)* —morally, ethically, economically, historically.
BOB	*(singing)* "Onward Christian soldiers, onward into war. With the cross of—"

SANDY Jesus, this kid won't shut up! David, you must remember what the good Lord said in the—Holy Land. "The poor are always with us. They got no fish, they got no loaves, and there's sweet bugger-all you can do about it." Fountains and libraries'll empty your pockets in six months. Sister Jane and the Sally Anns'll squander it puttin' herringbone suits on derelicts. If you want your dollars to go forth and multiply, the man to advise you is the gent who owns the egg-candling plant.

BOB What would you do, Mr. MacMillan, if you came into a sudden hundred grand?

  During the following, as SANDY *holds forth,* DAVID *wanders over to his table. He sits, deep in thought, holding the cable.*

SANDY Well, I'm already rich, so I think I'd be prodigal with it. I'd wait 'till the dead of winter, and I'd pack Beth off to Hawaii for a month. (*cupping his hands and calling out*) "Aloha, Elizabeth." Then I'd proceed, with a vengeance, to indulge my baser instincts.

HOWARD (*pouring another drink*) I'll need further fortification for this.

SANDY I've always had a private desire to sleep with three women at once.

BOB I've always wanted to sleep with one.

SANDY Really? You're still a virgin?

BOB I am. But I'm engaged.

SANDY Well, fornication's in your future. And if your apparatus is in order, you'll produce a wee bairn to carry your name.

MALCOLM And his name is Robert Ramsey!

SANDY Where was I?

TOM	In bed with three women.
SANDY	Tha's right. An' Beth's off doin' the hula in Hawaii. I'd take over Emma Day's for a whole damned month. I'd sate myself in sensual pleasure, playing' musical whores. I'd go through that house from cellar to rafters like a whirling dervish.
BOB	Mr. MacMillan, this is nasty. It's depressing me.
TOM	Rightly so.
SANDY	Kid, listen to an old practitioner of living. Life plays a lot of dirty little tricks, and most of them occur at the altar. *(near tears)* Oh, God, I hate it when the liquor makes me maudlin. I like it better when it makes me numb.
TOM	What's called for here is a toast to Daisy Gordon.
BOB	Who's Daisy Gordon?
MALCOLM	Robert Ramsey, Daisy Gordon was the mother of the Gordon brothers. They were exceptional curlers.
ANDY	Won four Buicks at a Bonspeil.
HOWARD	No curlers anywhere swifter with a broom.
TOM	*(lifting his glass)* Here's to Daisy Gordon's womb.
	All but DAVID *respond:*
ALL	"To Daisy Gordon's womb!"
	The stage darkens. The men ad lib, telling BOB *about the Gordon brothers. Light remains on* DAVID.
	Music comes up over the scene. Suggested music: "I'll Walk Alone."
	Curtain.

Act One, Scene Two

The back room, a week later. Seven a.m. DAVID is finishing his shave at the sink. HOWARD is sorting rakes in the back room. BETH MacMILLAN knocks on the front door of the Hardware.

BETH   Howard, open your doors!

HOWARD   Creepin' Ivy, who can that be? *(going to see)* It's Beth MacMillan.

DAVID   Wowsers. At seven in the morning.

HOWARD runs into the Hardware.

BETH   *(calling)* Howard?

HOWARD   *(unlocking the front door)* Good morning.

BETH   I thought you opened at seven.

HOWARD   Eight, actually. Is there something you need?

BETH   I'd like to talk to David.

She starts to move into the back room.

HOWARD   Are you pleased with your new interior?

BETH   Yes, thank you. The cabbage roses are gone.

She enters the back room; she has a headache, and is very nervous.

BETH	Good morning, David. I've come very early—really, inexcusably early—because I know you've been beset with visitors. Yesterday, apparently, you had a horde in here.
DAVID	It's unbelievable! All I do is sit in this room and *receive*. I feel like the Doge.
BETH	The Doge?
DAVID	You know, in the palace in Venice. The Doge had little compartments in the walls of his palace. People came and stashed petitions in the holes, and the Doge had to consider them.
BETH	Who is petitioning?
DAVID	They've come in swarms. The Canadian Girls in Training want a summer camp. The Golden Agers want a recreation room. The Oddfellows want a Burn Unit at City Hospital, and the Kiwanis sent a delegation for a new hockey rink. And persisting through all this is Howard's sister, Jane, preachin' that we'll all roast in hell with the Indians on our conscience. I have to say, Beth, I was happier last week, painting at your house.
BETH	*(controlling tears)* Were you, David? Were you happy last week?
DAVID	I was. It gave me distance from my money.

BETH *begins to cry.*

DAVID	Oh, my.
BETH	I'm sorry.
DAVID	You're... not well, are you?
BETH	I've got migraine. I've take so many two-twenty-twos, it's a wonder I'm not in a coma. I could use a spot of tea. Do you have something in the pot?

DAVID   *(getting a cup)* Yes, there's some leftover from breakfast.

BETH   Yesterday was bad, too. Mondays always are. Having to gear oneself up. Wondering how to occupy the week. *(taking the tea)* Thank you. *(a deep inhalation)* Something's gone haywire this year. Summers are usually better than winters. Winters are so silent, but in summertime the storm windows are off and the screens are on. I can hear birds chirping, neighbors mowing lawns, kids on bikes. Life comes into the house.

She again becomes weepy.

DAVID   Beth, what is it?

BETH   I'm so embarrassed. After you left, Friday, I spent the weekend trying to come up with some ruse. To get you back to the house. I cursed the damn Sweepstakes because, without that, I could have hired you to paint the second floor. And I wondered, David, why we go on this way. Both of us victims of past mistakes. Both of us so—marooned. We are marooned, aren't we?

DAVID   In different ways. You are—officially—attached.

BETH   I don't feel attached. I feel tethered, to an old certificate.

DAVID   Still, it's a reality.

BETH   Reality? This is yours, David, and look at it. Monks in cells live better. And my reality is Sandy MacMillan. In summers, if he's not at the golf club, he's at the whorehouse. In winters it's the curling rink or the whorehouse. He can't even father a child—

DAVID   *(embarrassed)* Now, Beth—

BETH   It's true! The doctor said it's him, not me. Something's wrong with Randy Sandy's sperm.

DAVID	Beth—
	DAVID *holds a finger to his lips, then points to an eavesdropping* HOWARD.
DAVID	*(raising his voice)* Howard's very busy with a new load of rakes.
BETH	*(loudly) I assume that he is.*
	HOWARD, *hurrying away, kicks a metal pail.*
BETH	Well, that's my reality. I've tried to talk to Sandy about adoption, but he won't hear a word of it. *(getting more tea)* David, it may look as if I'm standing here on the floor, but I'm far out on a limb. I'm dangling out here on this limb. I feel very raw, and I'm a little—doped—I think, from the pills, but the fact is that I, too, am here with a petition. *(brief pause)* Why can't we be comrades, David? Comrades in arms against time.
DAVID	*(finding this difficult)* Beth, many years ago Miss Logan persuaded me to join the library—
BETH	Oh, please, don't tell me to get a library card!
DAVID	I won't. But I've never forgotten what she said on that day. She said that lonely people were always at peril. We're like open wounds, waiting for all kinds of infection.
BETH	I'm nearly forty years old, David. I wash my face with milk every morning and then I rub it with cucumber. At night I smear on enough cold cream to grease a pig. *(she manages to laugh)* Heavens, I must be bonkers. Coming down here with rehearsed speeches, wondering if I'm still young enough to play the game. And then blurting out my worst fears about aging, when I came with seduction in mind.
DAVID	Where, Beth?

BETH   Where what?

DAVID   Where could we be comrades in arms? Would you
              have me crawl up a ladder, into Sandy's attic?
              Would we sneak off to some motel?

              A woman enters the Hardware. It is EMMA
              DAY. *We see her vaguely, being aware only
              that* HOWARD *is talking to a woman.
              Through the following,* EMMA *and*
              HOWARD *engage in serious conversation.*

BETH   *(whispering)* We have a little cabin at Loon Lake. I
              go there often, on weekends. Sandy never goes. We
              could drive up separately, and then—

DAVID   Beth, I can't.

BETH   *(without anger)* Surely you know, David, that of all
              the people in town, I have no designs on your
              money.

DAVID   I know that. And I can see that these feelings
              you're expressing run deep.

BETH   But you can't return them.

DAVID   I can't return them in kind. I don't want to be
              harsh, but I'm afraid if we took this invitation out
              to the sidewalk, it wouldn't stand up to the light of
              day.

BETH   *(sudden anger)* What it won't stand up to is your
              distorted memory of Mildred Douglas. You've
              taken an ugly, sordid incident, and packaged it up in
              rose-colored hindsight.

DAVID   I haven't! If I've packaged it, it's in a hair shirt. I
              lacerate myself with the damned thing.

BETH   Why? Need I remind you that you found the woman
              kissing Cammy Sinclair on the Five Corners with
              her blouse unbuttoned on the night before your
              wedding? *(a beat)* I shan't prolong this. I'll go now.

She gathers up her purse and sweater.

BETH   Do you know what migraine is, David? It's tears that won't come out. Blocked up, constipated tears.

EMMA DAY *enters. She wears a hat and dress; her gloves, handbag, and shoes are expensive. She wears little makeup and carries herself with aplomb.*

EMMA   Good morning, David.

DAVID   Emma Day!

EMMA   I'm sorry to interrupt—I see you have a guest.

DAVID   Yes. Uh, Miss Day, this is Mrs. MacMillan.

EMMA   I'm pleased to meet you. I'm always happy to welcome a newcomer to Raglan.

She pays scant attention to BETH, *and begins to examine* DAVID'*s quarters.*

BETH   I am not *new*. I'm the wife of Sandy MacMillan.

EMMA   I don't believe I know him.

BETH   Of course you do! Randy Sandy. He owns the egg-candling plant.

EMMA   I live on the outskirts of town, but I don't raise hens, so I don't sell eggs, and I have none to candle.

BETH   I was just saying goodbye to David. Goodbye, David.

DAVID   Goodbye, Beth.

EMMA   Goodbye, Mrs. MacGregor.

EMMA *finds a set of chrome faucets on a shelf. Nonchalantly, she turns one of them.*

BETH	Miss Day, my name is *MacMillan*. MacGregor's the Mayor.
EMMA	Is he? I thought old Graham was Mayor.
BETH	We buried old Graham two years ago.
EMMA	Did you? Goodness, I hope he was dead.

BETH moves out quickly, through the Hardware.

BETH	Goodbye, Howard.
HOWARD	G'bye, Mrs. MacMillan.

A moment passes, as EMMA *watches* BETH'*s exit.*

EMMA	She isn't aging well, poor slut.
DAVID	Emma, that's just damned harsh.
EMMA	Perhaps it is. I'm out of sorts this morning. I had a contretemps, as they say in Quebec, with my cook. *(removing her gloves)* The fruit man, the greengrocer, the butcher—they all add ten percent, and then the cook takes a kick-back. Cooks are the pimps of the kitchen.

Another customer enters the store: ANDY CAMPBELL *as "Dizzy Donohue."*

EMMA	David, I did not come here voluntarily. I was sent with a message for Howard.
DAVID	Really?
EMMA	Yes. Then I noticed Beth MacMillan on the premises, and I had a sudden, satanic urge to meet the woman. That is why I ventured into this appalling little billet of yours.
DAVID	It serves my needs.

EMMA   *(removing her hat)* It did in the past. But I hear
                you've hung up your brushes.

DAVID   Yes, I've retired.

EMMA   I suppose they're coming out of the woodwork like
                termites, now that you're floating in funds.

DAVID   What you said the first time I came to paint was
                true.

EMMA   What did I say?

DAVID   You said, "All the world's a marketplace."

                HOWARD *enters.*

HOWARD   S'cuse me, I've got an exchange. Fella bought a
                ten-foot extension cord when he needed a twenty.
                (finding the cord)

EMMA   Must be Dizzy Donohue.

HOWARD   'Tis.

EMMA   Try and sell him a measuring tape.

                HOWARD *exits.*

EMMA   David, I envy you your retirement. I'm past my
                prime. All my joints ache, and I frequently question
                my judgment. And lately— *(she wipes a tear)* Oh,
                dear, excuse me. *(finding a handkerchief)* Lately,
                tears come unannounced at the very mention of
                Graham.

DAVID   I'm sorry.

EMMA   I seldom come into town, since I attended his
                funeral.

DAVID   I didn't see you there.

EMMA   I stood behind a large maple. And the blanket of
            roses across the coffin was mine. Perhaps you
            knew that Graham and I shared a certain—
            fondness—for each other.

DAVID   I did know that.

EMMA   Graham was a grand old prairie socialist. He taught
            me this very valuable maxim: "The real test of a
            civilization is in the way it treats its poor."
            Graham kept the needy fed, the jail was empty, as
            were the welfare lists. Now we've got Malcolm
            MacGregor, ignoring the needy, throwing out trams
            for buses. And with his appointment of Andrew
            Campbell as Police Chief, we have kissed civil
            liberty goodbye. *(brief pause)* David, you must
            have heard the tale of Millie Douglas, skating on
            the river when she was ten years old?

DAVID   No, I don't recall—

EMMA   It was that bend in the river, close by my house.
            There'd been an early thaw, and she fell in, and I
            ran down and pulled her out.

            The customer leaves. HOWARD *disappears
            into the store.*

DAVID   Oh, yes. You took her in and gave her hot scones.

EMMA   Her parents wouldn't let her visit me. Due, of
            course, to the fact that I practise the horizontal
            profession. But I watched her grow from a distance,
            and we actually became pen pals. *(a deep
            inhalation)* What I'm about to say, David, is
            evidence of my questionable judgment. A month
            ago—this is very important—a month ago Millie's
            employer died, and she wrote me her plan to come
            home. She arrived in Raglan yesterday, and she's
            staying at my house.

DAVID   What? You—don't—mean—she's become a—

EMMA   She is a *guest*, David, at my house. A month ago
                she intended a visit to you. Today, she doesn't.

DAVID   That's impossible! How could she not—

EMMA   She arrived with no knowledge of your winnings!
                When I told her, I had to listen to what Mr.
                Shakespeare called "alarums and excursions." My
                God, what a clamor. She's leaving tomorrow
                morning, for the mountains.

DAVID   *(stunned)* Mountains?

EMMA   Some miles west of here there are large, geological
                protuberances called the Rockies. She's leaving for
                Banff in the morning.

DAVID   But why?

EMMA   David, one hundred and twenty thousand dollars is a
                vastly intimidating sum of money. These winnings
                of yours have given her a double handicap.
                Consider her position. She left under a large black
                cloud. Her reputation was in ruins. She's had
                fifteen rough years in Toronto, her youth is gone,
                and she's dirt poor. She screwed up her courage to
                come home because she expected to find you
                floundering, as she is, on the verge of middle-age.

DAVID   Oh, God, Emma. I am floundering!

EMMA   No. Suddenly you're a man of means. No one will
                believe that Millie's return, one week after the
                Sweepstakes, is coincidental. She will appear to be
                a golddigger. She *expected* to appear the prodigal
                daughter, coming home to atone. She expected
                she'd have to bootlick, because you held the moral
                high ground.

DAVID   Millie Douglas would never bootlick!

EMMA   David, there are throngs in town prepared to lick
                whatever you'd like.

DAVID	*(shocked)* Emma Day!
EMMA	I'm sorry. The language of my profession doesn't easily transfer to town. *(a beat)* I intuit, by the way, that even the MacMillan strumpet is up to skullduggery.
DAVID	Oh, not really—
EMMA	She was sniffing up your kilt, David, and don't deny it. The whole town is pandering to you. Millie refuses to join their ranks, and she refuses to see you. She does, however, want to see Howard.
DAVID	*Howard*??
EMMA	Yes. They were great chums in their youth. Apparently they met in a sandbox when Millie was two years old.
DAVID	Does he know she's back?
HOWARD	I've just told him.
DAVID	*(falling on a knee)* Emma, I'm on bended knee. Please, please, go back and plead a case for me.
EMMA	David, I won't plead your case because I've always thought your case a dubious one. For years, you know, I disliked you. I felt it so intensely, I actually considered hiring McGinty.
DAVID	McGinty paints barns.
EMMA	Yes. Unfortunately, he's a dripper. *(brief pause)* Mildred Douglas had what might be called a lapse. Granted, it was a serious one. Granted, it was the night before your wedding. Certainly, it called for confrontation. It did not call for the public spectacle of you sweeping through town with a horse-whip, shouting obscenities.

DAVID	Emma, if I could rip one page from the book of my life, that's the page I'd rip. *(running to his "wardrobe")* I'm gonna put on a tie and have that confrontation now!
EMMA	Stop where you are! You will not put on a tie. Mildred would have my head if she knew I'd betrayed her confidence.
DAVID	But you *have* betrayed her confidence!
EMMA	Yes, and I'll tell you why. You might not believe this, but I've managed to retain a romantic heart over the years. Against overwhelming odds, I might add. It was my romantic heart, in fact, that originally led me into—
DAVID & EMMA	*(simultaneously)* The horizontal profession.
EMMA	Yes. And although I won't plead a case for you, my romantic heart compels me to give you this golden opportunity. You can hie yourself down to the CN station tomorrow. You can sweep onto the platform and there, in the rather opulent manner of Russian literature, declare your love and make your amends.
DAVID	*(exasperated)* I can't do that! Not out in public, after fifteen years.
EMMA	Young man, if you don't—and I say this emphatically, David—if you don't, you will find yourself in the emergency room at City Hospital with multiple fractures. *(hollering)* Howard, come in here!
	HOWARD *enters.*
EMMA	Howard, I've been sent, as Millie's emissary, to invite you out to my house tonight.
DAVID	What??

HOWARD   Oh, Miss Day, that's impossible! If I were seen at
                your house, Jane'd make me lie on a bed of nails.
                Due, of course, to the fact that you practise—

EMMA &
HOWARD   *(simultaneously)* The horizontal profession.

EMMA   Yes. Well, I'm not surprised. In that case, why
                couldn't old Harry, my driver, deliver Mildred to
                your house tonight?

HOWARD   *(beside himself)* Oh, no! No, no, no. Jane'd have a
                coronary.

EMMA   Why would Jane have a coronary?

HOWARD   It has to do with the goalie.

DAVID   You don't mean... Cammy Sinclair?

HOWARD   Dear God, how can I say this? I never thought I'd
                have to. I'll try to put it in sequence. *(addressing
                DAVID)* The night before your wedding, you
                caught Millie with Cammy. The night before that,
                I caught Jane with Cammy!

EMMA   Bless us and save us!!

DAVID   Bloody horny bastard!

HOWARD   It's true. Jane was deflowered by Cammy Sinclair.
                She expected a marriage proposal the following
                day. That would be the day of the night before your
                wedding. But *that* night Cammy gets *Millie* into
                his car, and Millie loses her marbles, and you get
                the horse-whip, and the following day—that would
                be the day of your intended wedding—Cammy's
                gone to Toronto with Millie, and Jane's left a
                spinster. Mildred Douglas would not be welcome at
                my house.

EMMA   I see. Dear me, this is thick.

HOWARD	But we have an alternative. This here, where we are, is my second home. Harry can bring Mildred here tonight, and David will go spend the evening with Jane.
DAVID	This is lunacy! Emma, I mean no offense, but Millie didn't come back to Raglan for tea and scones. Howard, no offense meant, but she didn't come back to reminisce about the sandbox. I will not, after fifteen years of heartbreak, spend an evening discussing the scriptures with Jane!
HOWARD	*(heatedly)* Don't you dare belittle my sister!
DAVID	I wasn't! I—
HOWARD	*(fuming)* Jane's conversation isn't limited to the scriptures!
DAVID	I didn't say that—
HOWARD	There's more to Jane than meets the eye!
DAVID	*Apparently.*
HOWARD	Apparently? *(flexing his muscles)* McTavish, you wanna take this outside?
EMMA	Boys? Boys, please!
	HOWARD *pointedly swerves, turning his back to* DAVID. *He folds his arms and fumes for a moment. He addresses* EMMA, *in high dudgeon.*
HOWARD	Miss Day, would you please tell the house painter that—
DAVID	*(furiously)* I didn't paint *houses*, I painted *interiors*!!

HOWARD	*(to* EMMA*)* Please tell the painter that I'm determined to have this visit with Mildred.
DAVID	Howard—
HOWARD	*(to* EMMA*) Additionally*, he may have more money than Midas, but I'm the proprietor here, my name's on the deed, and I'm pullin' rank.
DAVID	But I'm the tenant! I've got a lease. I pay rent.
HOWARD	*(to* DAVID*)* Two bucks off the rent. Tonight, after the gents leave, you have to promise to—
EMMA	Swear to, David—
HOWARD	—go sit in my parlor with Jane.

He heads for DAVID'*s books.*

DAVID	What are you doing?
HOWARD	I want you to swear on this Bible. I want you to say, "I promise to visit Jane tonight between eight and eleven."
EMMA	Say it, David—and remember, this is an oath.
DAVID	I promise—
HOWARD	Put your hand on the Bible.
DAVID	*(doing so)* I promise to visit Jane tonight between eight and eleven.

We hear three toots from a car out front.

EMMA	That's Harry. He's wondering what's taking so long. *(she collects her hat and gloves)* Millie will be wondering, too. Tonight, Howard, I'll have Harry bring her up the alley to the back door.

HOWARD	I'd appreciate that. David, there's a delegation from Saskatchewan Handicapped, waitin' out on the sidewalk.

HOWARD exits to the store.

EMMA	*(as she follows)* Canada Bonds, David, Canada Bonds.
DAVID	Pardon?
EMMA	Put your money there. We don't approve of those who practice economic prostitution on the Yankee stock exchange. Goodbye.

She exits.

DAVID	Goodbye. *(pacing)* Oh, my God, I'm snookered. What'll I do? I've sworn on a Bible. And Emma called it an oath. Jesus, my nerves are raw. I'm gonna break out in shingles.

He goes to the "liquor" shelf, grabs his bottle, then halts abruptly.

Nope, too early. Much too early. *(pacing again)* Let's think about oaths. You take them at the altar. You take them in court. "The truth and nothing but the truth, so help me God." I took an oath to put my country first, in the Air Force. But, hell, that was war. *(he pauses, then looks at the ceiling)* So, help me, God. What'll I do? Surely you'd consider this promise more minor than major. Pardon? *(he listens)* Yes, I know. On a Bible. But does that have to make it *official*? It wasn't in church, or at City Hall, or in the military. I mean, is there a *flag* anywhere in this room? Was anyone wearing a clerical collar? Wasn't it just a little, expedient utterance in Howard's back room? Couldn't you have, in this particular instance, a little lenience? Pardon? *(he listens)*

> *We hear, quietly, the beginning of "What'll I Do?," a clarinet rendition.*

DAVID   Yes, I know, you've got rules. But rules are bent all the time. I'm not even asking you to bend. I'm asking you, please, to just—*tilt* a little. Couldn't you find it somewhere in your great, Godly heart, to tilt a little? *(a beat)* Pardon?

> *The music fills the theatre.* DAVID *keeps pleading, in his debate with God, although he can't be heard.*

> *Curtain*

> *End of Act One*

Act Two, Scene One

The evening of the same day. HOWARD *is excited. He finds a brown paper bag, takes out a bottle of good sherry, and opens it. He fetches two glasses and places them with the sherry. He hears a car at the back door.*

There is a knock at the back door. HOWARD *runs to open it.* MILDRED DOUGLAS *enters, prior to* EMMA DAY. EMMA *wears the same costume.*

HOWARD   Millie! *(hugging her)* Millie Douglas!

MILDRED   Oh, Howard, it's good to see you! You look wonderful.

HOWARD   Come in, come in. *You* look absolutely smashing. Miss Day, how are you?

EMMA   Frankly, I'm a bit snarky. We've got a contingent of snowplow salesmen at the house tonight. They're impossible to please in the summertime.

HOWARD   I didn't expect you.

EMMA   I'm not staying. I'm sending Harry back for Millie at ten o'clock. I just wanted to make sure everything was copacetic.

HOWARD   Everything is. He didn't even gather with the men. He left at four-thirty.

MILDRED   He was always as good as his word. *(near tears)* Unfortunately, I wasn't.

EMMA   *(sternly)* Mildred, wallowing in the past is wasteful. An Arab gent, out at the university, once gave me this advice: "The camel shits, and then the caravan moves on."

HOWARD   Millie, I hope you like sherry. I got some in.

MILDRED   Thank you, Howard.

EMMA   None for me, thank you.

MILDRED   *(examining the room)* Oh, my, this is where he lives.

EMMA   Where did he go at four-thirty?

HOWARD   Down to the *Raglan Maple Leaf.* He's cancelling his advertisement and announcing his retirement.

MILDRED   Howard, I hope you understand why I couldn't see him.

                  DAVID *is hiding in the trundle bed.*

DAVID   Why?

                  EMMA *and* MILDRED *think* HOWARD *asked the question.* HOWARD *is aghast.*

MILDRED   Because the Sweepstakes have— Howard, what's the matter?

EMMA   Goodness. It looks like severe stomach cramps.

                  The trundle bed wheels out from under the bench.

DAVID   *I* don't understand why you won't see me.

HOWARD   You lied! You're here!

MILDRED   Howard, you knew—

HOWARD   I did not!

MILDRED	Emma, you knew!
EMMA	I did not!
DAVID	They didn't. I swear they didn't.
EMMA	When *you* swear you might as well pass wind. You're a rotten, yellow-bellied rat!
DAVID	I know—
EMMA	You promised me!
DAVID	I know—
EMMA	And you swore on a Bible.
DAVID	What can I say? I'm a human catastrophe. *(taking a stance of authority)* Mildred, if I have my say, you will not go to the mountains tomorrow.
MILDRED	Listen to the man! If he has his say. Oh, the arrogance of the newly rich!

> DAVID *runs to the ice box and retrieves two dozen roses.*

DAVID	The newly rich have gifts! Mildred, this bouquet is a token of—
MILDRED	That bouquet isn't a token, it's a glut. I can't accept it.
DAVID	*(aggravated)* Why the hell not?
MILDRED	I'll tell you why!

> MILDRED *grabs the bouquet. She moves to an area where garbage pails and plastic buckets are stacked. There are three stacks. She dumps the roses, a few at a time.*

MILDRED	Because you're *flaunting* your money! *(she dumps a few)* Because it's the custom in Raglan to send *one* rose in a bud vase. *(she dumps again)* And surely it's excessive for a *tramp*— *(dumping again)* —and a *hussy.*
DAVID	Wait! There's even more excess! *(he runs to the ice-box and retrieves a huge, gold, heart-shaped box of chocolates)* Moyer's Deluxe chocolates.
MILDRED	Excessively deluxe. I won't accept those, either.
DAVID	Really? Well, how 'bout you, Emma? Would you like some chocolates?
EMMA	About as much as I'd like bubonic plague.
DAVID	*(to* HOWARD*)* Perhaps sister Jane?
HOWARD	No, thank you.
DAVID	*(angrily)* Well, they shouldn't go to waste. *(marching to the back door)* Some pedestrian might enjoy them. *(at the open door)* Hello? Pedestrians? Come and get 'em! *(he tosses the box out, and slams the door)*
EMMA	May I say, kiddles, that when calm goes out the window, calamity's at the curb. I did not come here to referee.
HOWARD	*(frightened)* I think I'd best go home to Jane.
EMMA	Mildred, what is your wish? To leave or to stay?
MILDRED	*(after a moment)* I'll stay.
EMMA	Very well. But I will neglect the snowplow gents, and wait outside in the car. If there is even a hint of abuse—scream. I'll send Harry in. You remember Harry, David? Harry is very large.
DAVID	Yes, Ma'am.

EMMA	Long on brawn and short on brain. '
DAVID	Yes, Ma'am.
EMMA	Known to react like a canine when I say "sic."
DAVID	Yes, Ma'am.
EMMA	You're forewarned.

> EMMA *and* HOWARD *start for the back door.*

DAVID	Howard, this had to be.
HOWARD	Not tonight, it didn't.
DAVID	I'll pay for the sherry.
HOWARD	Don't be daft. But not one red cent off the rent.
EMMA	*(at the door)* A rotten, yellow-bellied *sewer* rat.

> EMMA *and* HOWARD *exit through the back door.* MILDRED *and* DAVID, *now alone, are awkward together. A moment passes.*

MILDRED	I hear you flew a Spitfire during the war.
DAVID	*(a beat)* Yes, I did.

> *There is a pause.*

MILDRED	*(sadly)* The shoes are in my suitcase.
DAVID	The shoes?
MILDRED	The ones I'd planned to wear when we met. This isn't at all the way I intended it. I wanted to make an impression. I bought brand new shoes with Cuban heels. And nylon hose with a little pattern around the ankle. And a pretty print dress.

DAVID   You're very lovely as you are.

MILDRED   Thank you. I thought you'd be older, somehow, and bent from all the years painting baseboards. You're still very attractive.

DAVID   Thank you. But, Millie, on my insides I'm as dry as a ditch in July. How are you, on your insides? *(he awaits a reply)* Please, tell me. I want to know every detail. I don't care if it takes all night.

MILDRED   *(after a moment)* Fragile.

DAVID   That's it?

MILDRED   That's it.

DAVID   Millie, I'm not arrogant, I'm miserable. Last New Year's Eve I went to a party at the Mayor's house. I told Howard if I have to spend one more New Year's Eve singing "Auld Lang Syne" with no partner on my arm, I'll rev up my motor in his garage and die in a vapor of carbon monoxide. *(he awaits a response)* Many times, since you left—

MILDRED   I didn't leave, I was horse-whipped out of town.

DAVID   Many times, since your—departure—I've been at the end of my tether. I've suffered, for fifteen years, knowing that I ran the wrong person out of town.

MILDRED   David, everytime I see couples—children— families—I think, "There, but for Cammy Sinclair, go I." I was a human catastrophe long before you. May I try to explain?

DAVID   Please do.

MILDRED   I could do with a glass of that sherry.

DAVID   Certainly. *(he pours)*

MILDRED	I was in my room, trying on my bridal veil. I said to the mirror: "Mildred, you're nineteen years old, and you're very easy on the eyes." *(taking the glass)* Thank you. Then a queer feeling came over me. I leaned into the mirror, and my two pupils peered into the two, reflected pupils, and it was as if I was hypnotizing myself. *(gulping the sherry)* I thought, "You're nineteen, and tomorrow morning you're marrying David *forever*." Are you sure you want this in detail?
DAVID	I do.
MILDRED	"Forever." *(drinking again)* I remembered Mr. Monroe, in Grade Eleven, quoting us Macbeth's "tomorrow and tomorrow and tomorrow, to the last syllable of recorded time." I knew that meant forever. But that night the word was like a blow to the head. Like a concussion. I repeated it 'till I was almost in a trance. May I top this off?
DAVID	Certainly.
MILDRED	*(getting more sherry)* Dutch courage. David, this is the bald, unvarnished truth. I wanted, that night, to be with a stranger. I wanted to live the rest of my life with you, knowing there'd been, just once, someone else. I went out for a walk, and Cammy drove by and asked me into his car. I knew, if I didn't get in, I'd have spent the rest of my life wondering. What it would be like, with a stranger. That's the bald truth.
DAVID	I see. *(pouring himself more sherry)* Well, that's about as bald as truth ever gets. *(he drinks)* Where's Cammy now?
MILDRED	He's coaching a Pee-Wee hockey team somewhere. We parted ways after a year in Toronto. He wouldn't do at all, for the long haul. What about you?

DAVID   Oh, well, nothing much. A little dalliance in Watrous one time. A few trips out to Emma's. Nothing that ever engaged my feelings. What did you do in Toronto?

MILDRED   I sold hats for awhile, at Eaton's. Then I went to work for an old man, Mr. Dunlop. He'd been a Member of Parliament in his youth. He died a month ago, at eighty.

DAVID   Did he treat you well?

MILDRED   He was crippled and grouchy, and confined to a wheelchair. I got his meals and wheeled him around Queen's Park on nice days. And I read to him for an hour every evening.

DAVID   Did he like poetry?

MILDRED   No, the sweeping fictions. Dickens and Gallsworthy. He paid me little more than my board, but he had a pleasant house and I wanted for nothing. *(pause)* Nothing but you.

> *She begins to cry;* DAVID *goes to her and takes her in his arms.*

Oh, David, the years have been so lonely! I spent every Sunday in a deep depression.

DAVID   Oh, God, Sundays! The Hardware was closed, Howard was at home with Jane, and this back room felt like a dungeon. I'd wait all day for Jack Benny.

MILDRED   Amos 'n Andy.

DAVID   Charlie McCarthy. Mildred, I've loved you since I was seventeen.

MILDRED   Easter Sunday, when I was twelve, your folks gave you a big chocolate egg. You came to our gate and took the sugar flower off the top, and gave it to me. I've loved you since I was twelve.

They kiss.

DAVID *(very gently)* We could still have babies, couldn't we?

MILDRED Well, we'd have to be quick about it.

DAVID Please don't go to the mountains. Stay and be with me next Easter. Be with me New Year's Eve. Marry me.

MILDRED *(withdrawing from him)* David, until I learned about your winnings, I had a scenario all worked out. I thought, if we patched it up, I'd pry you out of this back room. I thought I'd help you channel your old fury into something positive. I thought you'd go off and work hard all day, and we'd get ourselves out, into the fray. Sit on committees, fight for the rights of the working class.

DAVID But why can't that still work?

MILDRED Because I relied on your being poor! Now you're retired. You've got half the town hounding you, pounding on your door, begging favors. And David, the Bible says, "Wealth maketh many friends." I wouldn't want friends like that. *(suddenly agitated)* I don't know what kind of life you're proposing. I can't even imagine what it would *mean* to be Mrs. McTavish. This is vital, David, because this would be *the long haul.* What are your plans for the money?

DAVID I haven't any.

MILDRED But you must have some inkling!

DAVID I haven't! I'd like to do something for the people of Raglan, but if I give to Howard's Indians, the Old Folks'll be mad. If I give to the Oddfellows, the Kiwanis'll be mad. No matter what I do, Sandy MacMillan'll have his knickers in a twist. My brain's gone on furlough and I can't sort it out.

MILDRED	So you imagine a life of philanthropy?
DAVID	I can't imagine anything but being with you!
MILDRED	Well, you're too young for the porch and rocker. And I really do believe that a man has no ballast without work. Isn't there, somewhere in your soul, some desire to strike out in a new direction?
DAVID	Yes, *marriage!* That would he my ballast. And then, together, we'd adjust to having money.
MILDRED	To what would we adjust?
DAVID	I don't know! I need more sherry. *(he goes for it)* Why are you badgering me like this?
MILDRED	Because I'm no longer nineteen! And I know, in my bones, that if I don't fit your plans, we're shooting ourselves in the foot.
DAVID	*(pouring sherry)* There was a time, 'bout five years ago, when I realized I didn't want to be doing hard, physical work when I was fifty. So I, uh— *(he drinks, proceeding with trepidation)* —I thought I'd actually like, well, some kind of an office. With, you know, *files*.
MILDRED	What would you do in the office?
DAVID	I don't know! Maybe something in business. But all the businessmen had loot to get launched, and I didn't. And I'd see 'em, chasing the buck, and they looked like a bunch of sharks. And I always felt like a minnow.
MILDRED	You used to be a man with strong, passionate opinions.
DAVID	I used to be a man who brandished a horse-whip! When you left, I buried that man.
MILDRED	And holed up, like a mole, in this room.

DAVID   Yes! Checked out. Sat on the sidelines.

MILDRED   Is that how you see us? Sitting on the sidelines?

DAVID   It's very safe on the sidelines! You don't get called a hot-head and a lunatic. And now I've got the loot to sit on the sidelines in luxury.

MILDRED   *(near tears)* David, we've had fifteen years of mutual misery. Now you want a commitment from me in the course of one summer evening. I can't do that. I can't chance a lifetime of misery, sitting on the sidelines, clipping coupons.

DAVID   Is that an ultimatum?

MILDRED   I suppose it is. If you want me to make that trip up the aisle, we'd have to resurrect some of our old dreams.

DAVID   God, what were they?

MILDRED   We were going to make a difference. Not because we wrote cheques to charities, but because we had a vision.

DAVID   Damnit, woman, visions come in shit-loads when you're young. Then life starts getting lived, and they dribble away. They just ooze out of you, year after year.

MILDRED   I don't believe that! When you're young, your visions are vague possibilities. But now, David, with a hundred and twenty thousand dollars, your visions could be *probabilities*. That's a luxury that happens to very few people. *(going to the door, calling out)* Emma? I'll be right there.

DAVID   You can't leave now! We've got to settle this.

MILDRED *gathers her hat and purse.*

MILDRED   No, David, *you* have to get in touch with your visions. You have to settle on a new occupation. Please, try and understand. One more failure would kill me.

DAVID   And *you've* got to understand that I've lived my life with no choices! No alternatives. I've only lived one week with money!

MILDRED   That's why I'm going to Banff in the morning.

DAVID ·   You can't!

MILDRED   I'll come around early, to say goodbye.

DAVID   Mildred, this is just damned cruel! You're leaving me here like a beached whale.

MILDRED   I'll be gone for two weeks. That gives you time to search your soul and find a goal. If you find one, I'll come back. If you don't, I won't. Goodnight.

> MILDRED *exits.* DAVID *stands paralyzed, inhaling and exhaling.*

DAVID   Well, ain't this the cat's pajamas? *(he drinks and ponders the glass)* This sherry is a piss-poor excuse for a drink. *(going to a shelf)* I need the real McCoy. I need a whole damn bottle of the Mayor's Crown Royal.

> *He takes the bottle and the glass to center-stage, and looks to the ceiling.*

Sir? It's me again. I hope your line isn't busy. If you don't mind my saying so, you made a big omission. Way back, years ago, when you performed that business in the Holy Land. Pardon? *(he listens)* Yes, I *can* be more specific. I'm talking about the business with the rib, in the Garden of Eden. *Big omission.* When you made women, you didn't give the men a clue. *(he drinks)* I mean, here I am, the John D. Rockefeller of the prairies. I

could buy her a diamond at Birks. I could buy her
furs at Yaeger's. But what does she want? She
wants to know how I'm gonna occupy myself
between nine and five! Pardon? *(he listens)* Yes, I
do have a request. What I need tonight is a
revelation. Because I want this woman tomorrow
and tomorrow and tomorrow. Until the last syllable
of recorded time. And revelations, Sir, are up to
you.

> *Music up. Suggested music: "I Love You
> So Much It Hurts Me."*

> *Curtain.*

Act Two, Scene Two

> *The back room of* HOWARD'*s Hardware,
> early morning, the following day.* DAVID *is
> asleep, fully clothed, on his trundle bed. He
> has removed his tie and unbuttoned his shirt.
> His liquor bottle is beside the trundle.*

> HOWARD *unlocks the front door of the
> Hardware and moves quickly to the back
> room. He is anxious, not knowing* DAVID'*s
> state of mind.*

HOWARD   Yoo-hoo. *(*DAVID *groans)* Good morning.

DAVID   Good morning.

HOWARD   Is it? Or do we still have the threat?

DAVID   What threat?

HOWARD   You, in my garage, dead of carbon monoxide.

DAVID   She's going to Banff this morning.

> HOWARD *gets the bottle and takes it back to the shelf.*

HOWARD   So this, then, was to drown sorrows.

DAVID   She's stopping in shortly, to say goodbye. She says she loves me, but she wants me to find a new occupation.

HOWARD   Well, Jumpin' Juniper, David, that's a piece-a-cake! You say repeatedly—in fact, tediously—that there's posterity in books. Why don't you open a bookstore?

DAVID   No, I'd like to aim a little higher. Do you mind my asking, Howard, have you ever had an aspiration?

> HOWARD *gets a dolly and begins to load paint cans on it.*

HOWARD   Whaduyuh mean?

DAVID   You've been selling hardware since you were sixteen. Have you ever aspired to anything else?

HOWARD   *(plunking a can)* Never had to. When I inherited the store, I was guaranteed three squares a day. I keep my nose clean, and I keep my clean nose to the grindstone.

DAVID   But haven't you ever harboured some secret fantasy?

HOWARD   One.

DAVID   What's that?

HOWARD   It's embarrassing.

DAVID   Please, tell me.

HOWARD	*(sheepishly)* Once a month, in my dreams, I'm Fred Astaire. I'm puttin' on my top hat, puttin' on my white tie, puttin' on my tails. I do all that at home. Then I come into the Hardware, and I dance with rakes and spades and mops. I tap, tap, tap on top of paint cans. I dance all over the ceiling.
DAVID	You want to be a movie star?
HOWARD	*(plunking a can)* No, I just wanna dance like Fred for five minutes.
DAVID	*(stealing himself)* Howard, do you really think we've got a pack of donkeys on the Council?
HOWARD	To a man.
DAVID	But they've all been to university.
HOWARD	Donkeys with diplomas, to a man.
DAVID	Tell me honestly if this is Maniac McTavish gone raving mad. Do you think I'd have a hope in hell if I ran for Council?
HOWARD	*(dropping a can)* City Council?
DAVID	Yes.
HOWARD	Shit, man, I'm gonna blow a gasket!
DAVID	Is it just a pipe dream?
HOWARD	You'd be a vital presence at that table!
DAVID	But I haven't any skills!
HOWARD	That makes you qualified. Oh, man, this is exciting!
DAVID	And I don't know anything about "Robert's Rules of Order." What the hell is "Robert's Rules of Order"?

HOWARD	Calm down, David! It's sort of an "Emily Post" for politicians. Instructions for the proper conduct of meetings.
DAVID	Would it he at the library?
HOWARD	I'm sure it would.
DAVID	*(pacing)* I feel altogether unhinged!
HOWARD	David, Malcolm MacGregor says a man must have a name that's known. For twenty years your ad's appeared in the *Maple Leaf*, keeping your name before the public. You've carried your ladder into nearly every residence in Raglan, so you've practically got a ready-made constituency.
DAVID	That's the general populace. What about my opponents? Two of 'em are sharks. What if I'm just bait for the sharks?
HOWARD	Who are you worried about?
DAVID	Frank, at Frank's Furniture; and Bill at the bicycle shop.
HOWARD	David, 'member what Mr. Roosevelt said? You've got nothing to fear but fear itself. *(stopping the loading)* Frank and Bill have a lot of enemies, and you have none. They've got swelled heads from power, and bloated bellies from privilege. *You're* clean as a whistle, fresh as a daisy. And Frank and Bill are out fundraising 'till the cows come home. You've got endless resources. You'd be a shoe-in!

There is a knock on the back door.

DAVID	Oh, God, that's Mildred!
HOWARD	I say full speed ahead and damn the torpedoes! Tell her you're going to run.

DAVID *opens the door to* MILDRED *and* EMMA. MILDRED *wears her "outfit," as previously described. She is sad, and she enters without touching* DAVID.

MILDRED   Good morning.

DAVID   Good morning.

MILDRED   Good morning, Howard.

HOWARD   Morning, Mildred. Miss Day.

EMMA   Good morning.

MILDRED   Howard, I'm afraid we can't have our visit. This is a very sad occasion.

HOWARD   It needn't be. David has a piece of news.

DAVID   Mildred, is this the special outfit?

MILDRED   It is.

DAVID   Well, it's just swell.

MILDRED   Thank you.

HOWARD   David has a piece of news.

DAVID   The dress is nice, and the nylons are spiffy, and the shoes are nifty, but what's best is the lady inside.

EMMA   The lady inside is on her way to the train station.

HOWARD   Not necessarily. David has a piece of news.

EMMA   So you keep saying. *(to* DAVID*)* Perhaps you could share it, since the trains run on time.

DAVID   Mildred, I know what I want to do for the people of Raglan. I want to run for Council.

EMMA	City Council?
DAVID	Yes.
EMMA	*(amazed)* Great saints!
MILDRED	Do you mean professional politics?
DAVID	Yes! Can you take that much fray?
MILDRED	*(very surprised)* Oh, David, this is much more than I'd bargained for.
EMMA	What's your agenda?
DAVID	My what?
EMMA	Your platform!
DAVID	I'll get one—toot sweet, as they say in Quebec.
EMMA	*(in frustration)* Well, you can't even *think* of running without one?
DAVID	*(irritated)* Damnit, Emma, thoughts don't always come in paragraphs! This one came in a sentence. It had a period after it. *(he pretends that he's writing the sentence)* "I want to run for Council." *(when he gets to the period, he pokes it and says "phfft"; he turns to* MILDRED*)* What do you think?
MILDRED	I think you'd be magnificent. I think you'd get in there and really *represent*. But Mr. Dunlop said that in politics the men dismember each other while their wives serve tea. Would I just preside over a teapot?
EMMA	First thing you'd do is get a platform.
DAVID	Mildred, I couldn't, in a million years, do this alone. You'd have to be there, by my side, resurrecting the dreams, putting them into practice.

MILDRED	*(going to him)* David, if you really, really want this, I'll be there like glue.
DAVID	Then a Councilman's wife is the life I'm proposing! Will you now, please, accept my hand in marriage?
MILDRED	*(kissing him)* I will.
HOWARD	Yippee!
	MILDRED, *laughing, goes to hug* EMMA. HOWARD *hugs* DAVID, *then* MILDRED.
DAVID	*(excitedly)* We could take full-page ads in the *Maple Leaf.* We could, if Howard agrees, retain this back room for my campaign headquarters.
HOWARD	I agree!
DAVID	We could put a big bunting across the store: "David McTavish for Council—no muss no fuss." And I can recruit at least fifty volunteers.
HOWARD	*(excitedly)* A hundred, Davey! And they'd be bound to buy something, comin' in or goin' out.
EMMA	Prior to all that, kiddles, you need a platform!
MILDRED	We'll sit in the park this afternoon and write one.
	A customer, BOB RAMSEY *in disguise, enters the store and rings the counter bell.*
HOWARD	*(getting the dolly)* But, David, you mustn't dally. The elections are 'round the corner and the other candidates have a head start. Hie yourself down to City Hall and register.
	He exits to the store.
DAVID	I will! We'll go this morning. Emma, why don't you come with us?

EMMA   If I presented myself at City Hall, they'd all drop dead. My transactions with City Hall take the form of cash, delivered to our Police Chief in small, brown paper bags. I'm going down to the pharmacy. Fitzsimmons is mixing a potion for my arthritis. *(to* DAVID*)* Now, obviously, David, there's no need for me to contribute to your campaign. But I might assist in another way. Are you aware that two of your opponents are the scum of the earth?

DAVID   I am.

EMMA   Are you aware that both have skeletons in their closets?

DAVID   No, I'm not.

EMMA   Well, I am. If things get ugly, I wouldn't be above a little skeleton-rattling. Mildred, when you put your heads together on the platform, you'll have to come up with something extraordinary. It can't be the same old malarkey. It must be unique, to the two of you. It must, in fact, be dazzling. *(at the door)* David, your thought that ended with the period was a good one. If you play your cards right, you could be an island of reason in a sea of thieves. Goodbye.

> *She exits.* DAVID *grabs* MILDRED. *They become giddy.*

DAVID   I'd have an office *and* files!

MILDRED   And three-piece suits, Harris tweed!

DAVID   And a watch with a fob, and a Parker pen in my hand!

MILDRED   And a Ronson lighter on a big, mahogany desk!

> BETH MacMILLAN *enters the Hardware.*

BETH   Good morning, Howard. Is Millie here?

HOWARD	Yes, actually—

BETH *moves into the back room.*

BETH	Oh, Mildred, I'm glad I found you. Do you remember me? I used to be Beth Stewart.
MILDRED	*(shaking hands)* I remember you very well. And I remember your dad's smithy.
BETH	Do you?
MILDRED	Very warmly. When I was eight, I had a Pinto pony that needed shodding. Times were hard and your dad did it free.
BETH	He was generous that way. Millie, I'd appreciate it very much if we could talk privately. I thought we might have coffee up the street at the Greek's.
MILDRED	Actually, David and I—
BETH	I'm sorry to impose, but this really is an urgent matter. Perhaps we could just step into the back alley for a few minutes?
DAVID	Heavens, no. We can't have you chatting out there with the tomcats and the trash. Millie, I have a little business at City Hall. I'll go do that, while you two chat right here.
BETH	That's good of you, David. Thank you.
DAVID	*(kissing MILDRED)* I'll be back soon.
MILDRED	Godspeed.
DAVID	And Mum's the word.
MILDRED	Of course.

DAVID *exits through the store. The
customer leaves. The women are now
slightly uncomfortable with each other.*

BETH	So. Is there to be a wedding?
MILDRED	Yes, there is.
BETH	Will it be a white one?
MILDRED	No, I don't think that would be appropriate. *(pause)* You had a white wedding, didn't you?
BETH	I did. *(squirming)* Mildred, I'm here—quite humbly, really—because I think you have knowledge of a mistake I made in my teens.
MILDRED	Beth—
	MILDRED *gestures to* HOWARD, *in the store. He is hovering too closely.*
MILDRED	*(loudly)* Howard's very busy in the store.
BETH	*(loudly) I assume that he is.*
	HOWARD *moves away, again kicking a pail.*
BETH	This has been my military secret, because white was not, in my case, appropriate either.
MILDRED	Beth, he told me.
BETH	I thought he might. *(brief pause)* Cammy Sinclair went through this town like a dose of salts. *(pleadingly)* May I, please, rely on your silence?
MILDRED	You may.
BETH	Thank you. I'll be eternally grateful. *(after a pause)* He wasn't much, was he? I mean, he pranced about like a stallion, but he wasn't much, was he?
MILDRED	Not much at all, when push came to shove.
BETH	*Especially* when push came to shove!

They both laugh. SANDY *enters through the back door.*

SANDY — Mildred, welcome back to—oh. Beth. This is a surprise. Hello.

BETH — Hello, Sandy.

SANDY *shakes* MILDRED'*s hand.*

SANDY — Mildred, glad to have you back.

MILDRED — Thank you.

SANDY — What was all the chuckling about?

MILDRED — A shared experience, from the past.

SANDY — *(looking for* DAVID*)* David's not here?

MILDRED — He had to run an errand.

SANDY — Well, I've got a hot tip. I wanted to pass it on, since he's now a certified member of the brass.

MILDRED — And he's soon to be my husband. Can you trust it to me?

SANDY — Absolutely. Mildred, money has become, as they say in Quebec, my "raisin detter." Right now we've got a post-war boom and property is the ticket.

MILDRED — Yes, we'll have to buy a house.

BETH — Millie, Sandy's talking about real estate. The subdivision of real estate. *(to* SANDY*)* I thought we were playing this close to the chest.

SANDY — Elizabeth, one thing this prairie's got is lots and lots of prairie. I made my own purchase early this morning. *(to* MILDRED*)* Mildred, subdivision's the ticket to riches. They're leaving the farms in droves and pouring into the city with no place to live.

BETH	*(confidentially)* This is classified information, so keep it under your cap.
SANDY	Millie, I've had my ear to a wall. The Council's proposing a blacktop highway all the way out Avenue A.
MILDRED	Oh, that'll be easier on the vehicles, won't it?
BETH	What that means, Mildred, is that Raglan's going to develop north, out Avenue A.
SANDY	The old Hogarth farm is on Avenue A. It's two-hundred acres, and it's on the market dirt cheap.
BETH	Dirt cheap because Hogarth isn't part of the brass, and he never has his ear to a wall.
SANDY	So you must tell David to focus on *subdivision.*
MILDRED	You mean selling it off bit by bit?
BETH	Acre by lucrative acre.

SANDY *offers* MILDRED *a business card.*

SANDY	Here's my sister Edith's card. She's a real estate agent on the Five Corners. She's handling the property.
MILDRED	Sandy, I can't speak for David, but I don't think subdivision's quite our dish of tea. But, thank you. It'll give us some fodder for thought. *(pause; she looks at them)* You two make quite a grand team.

BETH *and* SANDY *are embarrassed at the compliment. They are unable to look at each other.*

MILDRED	You know, they say fools rush in where angels fear to tread. I'm going to rush in—and I apologize in advance, because you might think I'm brash.

SANDY   You're bound to be, after fifteen years in Toronto.
           What's on your mind?

MILDRED   Have you ever considered adoption?

BETH   *(awkwardly)* Millie, I guess you don't know that
           our marriage has been on the rocks for some years
           now.

MILDRED   Well, that's not unusual. Married couples tend to
           get very sloppy with each other. But it's never too
           late to make another stab, is it?

BETH   I'm prepared to listen, if Sandy is.

SANDY   Proceed.

MILDRED   Emma Day's told me of a sad situation. There's a
           fifteen-year-old girl in town, four months pregnant.
           She's going to put the child up for adoption.

SANDY   Oh, boy. Mildred, here's the rub. You never know
           what the hell you're going to get with adoption.

MILDRED   This girl's father's on the board at the Wheat Pool.
           He's widowed now, but it was a fine, upstanding
           family.

SANDY   That's the mum. I mean, you've got your ewes and
           then you've got your rams. The ram coulda been
           some derelict gypsy, riding the rails, passin'
           through town on a CN freight car.

MILDRED   Actually, the ram is in his first year of university.
           He's studying physics.

BETH   Isn't that like mathematics?

SANDY   No, Beth, it isn't. Physics is "E equals mc
           squared."

BETH   Oh. That's good to know.

MILDRED	It seems to me this child has very fine credentials.
BETH	*(pleadingly)* Sandy, please don't slam the door on this. You always say that a smart businessman leaves the door ajar.
SANDY	Oh, boy. Trouble is, smart businessmen ain't necessarily good dads. A good dad'd have to... severely limit his... extra-curricular activities. Still, these blood lines don't sound half bad. *(to BETH)* Tell yuh what let's do. Let's you and me go up to the Greek's and have lunch.
BETH	Oh, I'd love that. I'd love us to be seen together publicly. I mean, I'd love for the public to see—
SANDY	Beth, I know. I know it ain't been easy. But let's not get maudlin. *(starting out)* Mildred, if you want your dollars to go forth and multiply, you'll make a swift offer on the Hogarth farm.
MILDRED	I'll tell David.
BETH	Elizabeth, come along.
BETH	Goodbye, Millie. And Millie— *(taking her hand)* —even though you left with your reputation in tatters, I'd like to assure you that if you invite us to dinner, we'll come. And of course, if *we* come, everyone will.
MILDRED	Thank you.
SANDY & BETH	Goodbye. 'Bye. G'bye, Howard.

> SANDY *and* BETH *go out through the Hardware.* MILDRED *reads the business card.* HOWARD *comes in immediately.*

HOWARD	Holy Hollyhocks! The MacMillans walked outta my store together.
MILDRED	Yes, they're quite a pair, aren't they?

HOWARD	I know what's wrong with Sandy. He can't sire a child. But do you know what's wrong with Beth?
MILDRED	What?
HOWARD	She didn't get enough Planter's Peanuts in her youth.
	MILDRED, *bewildered, frowns at* HOWARD.
MILDRED	Planter's Peanuts?
HOWARD	I didn't get it, either.
	DAVID *bursts in, joyously.* EMMA, *flustered, follows him.*
DAVID	I'd like you to meet a fella who just registered for Council!
MILDRED	*(embracing him)* Congratulations!
HOWARD	Hallelujah!
EMMA	David, what is this about? *(to* MILDRED *and* HOWARD*)* The man bolted into the pharmacy, knocked down a whole shelf of Carter's Little Liver Pills, and dragged me back here!
DAVID	Because I've got a proposition. Millie, visions are swarmin' like grasshoppers in August. *(pacing with glee)* I was on cloud nine, walking up to City Hall, and suddenly I remembered what my old dad used to say: "Shelter first." Millie and I will need a house, and I don't think we want one of the little war-time boxes. I think we'd like something away from the center, with some land and some horses. Now, Millie, hang onto your hat. You too, Howard. Emma's been hinting at retirement for some time now. Emma, if you'd be prepared to sell, I'd be prepared to buy.

> EMMA, HOWARD, *and* MILDRED *react simultaneously.*

HOWARD   Jumpin' Juniper!

MILDRED   What?

EMMA   I beg your pardon?

DAVID   Mildred, confirm for me that you love Emma's house.

MILDRED   Every inch of it, but—

DAVID   So do I! You've been cooped up with a stingy old man; I've been on a trundle with a hot plate. Maybe, after all we've been through, we have a right to a smashing house.

MILDRED   David, this is hasty! We'd all need to sleep on it.

EMMA   I've no need to sleep on it.

HOWARD   Miss Day, you'd need to consider a fair price.

EMMA   I know the fair worth. David, this idea is fresh and original. Assure me, please, that this idea originated with you.

DAVID   Of course it did! Fifteen minutes ago.

EMMA   If I thought for a moment that someone was trying to shut down my house, I'd resort to nasty tactics. *(to* HOWARD*)* If I thought that someone's self-righteous sister was doing dirt to my girls, there'd be civil war in Raglan.

HOWARD   Miss Day, my sister saves souls, and I sell hardware. Ideas like this are never conceived by people like us.

EMMA   Right you are. *(a beat)* Actually, the idea of Millie
              and David residing in my house is most appealing.
              (to MILDRED*)* I've always loved you, and David—
              well, David is one of those acquired tastes. But I
              should warn you that my terms will be steep and
              intractable. This is, after all, business.

DAVID   I'd hoped, Emma, that we might conduct this as
              friends.

EMMA   I'm afraid not. If we come to an agreement, we'll
              celebrate as friends. *(she moves into her tough
              "negotiation" mode)* The house comes with ten
              acres of land, and it can't be touched for less than
              twenty thousand. That figure is not negotiable.

HOWARD   That figure is highway robbery! You can buy a
              fine, modern house with all the latest fixtures for
              less than ten thousand.

EMMA   Howard, modern houses are without embellish-
              ment, without style or charm, and they're thrown
              together with a lick and a promise. Fine modern
              houses have crappy chrome faucets, purchased from
              your Hardware, rather than solid brass. Fine modern
              houses have nothing to recommend them but
              picture windows, in front of which mindless,
              modern people, by some sort of silent consensus,
              place large, vulgar table lamps. My house was
              built by artisans. They were hired by a British
              baronet who fled to Canada in 1912, when caught
              in flagrante in a public toilet with a British
              Horseguard. Twenty thousand.

                        *Another customer enters the Hardware and
                        rings the bell.*

DAVID   Mildred, let's agree to twenty.

HOWARD   You can't! Mildred—

MILDRED   Howard, David is at the helm, and I approve.

HOWARD	He may be at the helm, but he's got grasshoppers on the brain. *(to* DAVID, *as he goes)* You're goin' through your money like poop through a goose.

He exits to the store.

EMMA	Unfortunately, I can't let it go for twenty because I have moral debts.
MILDRED	Moral debts?
EMMA	I have a staff of five. What do you imagine will happen to my girls?
MILDRED	Wouldn't they just find themselves another house?
EMMA	The two young ones would, but three have long seniority. They're too old to begin again elsewhere, and I won't turn them out. And there is, you see, a ghost looming over us.
DAVID	The ghost of whom?
EMMA	Old Graham. *(looking to the ceiling)* He's up there watching, in the socialist's corner of Heaven. Some years ago Mayor Graham came to visit me—he was a stranger at the time. He inquired, very politely, if I'd made any pension provision for my girls. I hadn't, but I found the idea very enlightened. We discussed it awhile, and then, of course, he stayed for dinner. Graham's very last word to me, on his deathbed, was "reparations."
DAVID & MILDRED	Reparations?
EMMA	It has two definitions: One—a compensation for wrong or injury. Two—a compensation for devastation of territory. I'll use Lizzie as an example. Lizzie Evans, after a dozen years tending to Randy Sandy MacMillan, is devastated territory.
DAVID	You want me to pay for Lizzie's pension?

EMMA   I do. Handsomely. Three thousand.

DAVID   Wowzers!

MILDRED   David, Lizzie did sell you the Sweepstakes ticket.

EMMA   Lizzie's had a lifelong dream of going out to
Vancouver Island and raising mushrooms. I mean
to see that dream realized.

MILDRED   Three thousand for Lizzie seems fair to me.

EMMA   Good. I will personally give a generous severance
to my two young ones. But Martha Currie and Kate
McGuire—

DAVID   Emma, this *is* verging on highway robbery!

EMMA   It isn't robbery, it's parity. Martha Currie and Kate
McGuire have been with me eighteen years. I have
pictures of them when they joined me in 1930.
They were flawless beauties. Today they carry on
their faces not only the ravages of time, but also
wrong and injury. One thousand each for Martha
and Kate.

DAVID   Emma, you may be arthritic, but you're not deaf.
This moral debt of yours is *not my responsibility*.

EMMA   Of all the politicians who've served in your
lifetime, who would you most like to emulate?

DAVID   Well, obviously, old Graham.

EMMA   What we're doing here today is paying homage to
Graham. One thousand each, for Martha and Kate.

MILDRED   That would bring us to twenty-five.

DAVID   And twenty-five is my limit.

EMMA   However—

DAVID   No, Emma. No *however*!

EMMA	But my gardener, Duncan—
DAVID	Duncan Walsh sells bootleg whisky! He's got a bundle in the bank.
EMMA	But my driver, old Harry, hasn't.
DAVID	*(emphatically)* Old Harry's already got a pension from the Post Office! I am telling you, finally, I've got zip in my coffers for Harry.
EMMA	*(caving in)* Very well. We'll put it to bed at twenty-five. Is that satisfactory?
DAVID	It is.

MILDRED *is suddenly sad.*

MILDRED	Oh, my.
DAVID	*(shaking* EMMA*'s hand)* Emma, I've just moved from cloud nine to seventh heaven.
EMMA	*(noticing* MILDRED*)* Mildred, what's wrong?
MILDRED	*(tearfully)* Nothing. Really, I'm fine.
EMMA	No, something is stinking in Denmark. What is it?
MILDRED	I can't imagine Raglan without you. Where will you go?
EMMA	I'll go home to my birthplace in Weyburn. I'd like to have my bones buried there, alongside my mother. In the meantime, I'll volunteer part-time, at the mental asylum.
DAVID	The mental asylum's a madhouse!
EMMA	*(to* MILDRED*)* I can't believe he said that. *(she is tired; she falters, swaying slightly)* Oh, dear. Goodness me.
MILDRED	Are you all right?

EMMA	Kiddles, I am world-weary. I'm as world-weary as one can get after forty years in Raglan.
	MILDRED *helps her into a chair. Another customer, "Dizzy Donohue," enters the store.*
	Thank you. I must say, it's a little sad, breaking up the gang. We always closed on Sundays, and in the old days Graham would visit. We'd go down to the riverbank and light a bonfire and roast potatoes. I can't carry a tune in a bucket, but Graham and Martha Currie could've held their own in any concert hall. They used to sing "The Skye Boat Song." *(she hums the first two lines)* Graham called us "The Campfire Girls." Ah, well, Graham's gone. And so are all the shy, young men. They went off to the war innocent farm boys, and they came back—the ones who came back—were bold and brittle. All the ceremony's gone out of it.
	She rises, gathering strength. HOWARD *comes in, hurriedly.*
HOWARD	S'cuse me. I've got an exchange. *(he looks for a box)*
DAVID	Dizzy Donohue.
HOWARD	Yessireebob. Bought long-nose pliers when he needed slip joint.
DAVID	Howard, we've reached an agreement.
HOWARD	Leapin' Lilacs. Twenty thousand?
EMMA	Twenty-five, actually. David is helping me pension off the girls.
HOWARD	What? That's outrageous!
EMMA	Solid brass, fixtures, Howard. Solid brass fixtures.

HOWARD Miss Day, chrome may be crappy, but it doesn't tarnish.

EMMA I know that, Howard. It just sits there and offends.

HOWARD *leaves with the pliers.*

EMMA Now, I'd like to expedite the paperwork quickly. I'll go up the street to see Harrison Esquire. We can be out in a month. *(at the door)* I can't think of two people who'd be better stewards of my house. I give you both my blessing. *(she looks to the ceiling)* Graham, I think I handled this most equitably. I hope you do, too.

EMMA *exits.* DAVID *embraces* MILDRED.

DAVID May I make a formal invitation?

MILDRED Please do.

DAVID David Kenneth McTavish, invites Mildred Moira Douglas, to join him at six o'clock this evening, when they will announce, to the gathering, their purchase of property.

MILDRED *And* their dazzling political platform!

They kiss. Music up. Suggested music: "Oh, Look At Me Now."

Curtain

Act Two, Scene Three

It is five-thirty the same day. HOWARD *is in the Hardware, the back room is empty. There is a quick knock on the back door and* TOM WALLACE *enters, chuckling.*

TOM *(calling into the Hardware)* Howard, I'm early. Shut the shop!

HOWARD *(calling back)* Not 'till six.

TOM *(going for his bottle)* I wanna celebrate the sale of the century!

HOWARD Not 'till six. Help yourself to a drink.

TOM I am.

MALCOLM MacGREGOR *enters from the back door. He is in a daze.*

MALCOLM Oh, my God, heavy lies the head that wears the crown. Howard, pour me a drink.

TOM Malcolm, I'm Tom. Howard's still in the store.

MALCOLM *goes to a shelf numbly, without looking at* TOM.

MALCOLM Thomas, you're lookin' fit as a fiddle.

TOM Thank you. You're lookin' like death warmed over.

MALCOLM *pours his Crown Royal.*
ANDY CAMPBELL *enters from the alley.*

ANDY	Oh, lads, this is thick! Thick, thick, thick. The upstart's bought out Emma Day! Lock, stock, and barrel!
TOM	*(happily)* Not the stock, Andy! He's turning the ladies out to pasture with a pension.
ANDY	*(getting his drink) I* think his motivation is rooted in pinko thinking!
TOM	Pinko thinking?
ANDY	He's been dangling out there, left of center, for years. The man's turned traitor against the brass of the town!
TOM	Oh, Andy, why dontcha go out an tag a few cars?
ANDY	What'll happen to the travelling salesmen at the King Edward? Where'll they go without the whorehouse? What about Neilson's Department store? Those whores spent a mint on clothes.
TOM	And what'll happen to your extortion?
ANDY	Thomas, extortion's a very harsh word.
TOM	Harsh, but apt. Emma operated unhindered under Graham, then you went out with your goons and broke her windows. Emma Day's money flowed like the Ganges into the cop shop.
MALCOLM	And McTavish has dammed up the river. I thought I knew that man like the back o'me hand. *(an impassioned lament to the heavens)* God in Heaven, who the hell am I, if I don't know people?
ANDY	Malcolm, watch the blood pressure. Your eyes are buggin' out.
MALCOLM	Don't patronize me, copper! I'm the man who took you off the beat and made you part of the brass.
TOM	*(pulling up a chair)* Malcolm, park yourself.

MALCOLM *sits. Someone knocks at the door.*

TOM   Randy Sandy. Why's he knockin'? Come in!

BOB RAMSEY *enters.*

BOB   *(to* TOM*)* Mr. Wallace, I wondered if I might be
               allowed to gather?

TOM   Of course you're allowed.

BOB   Thank you. *(displaying a bag)* I brought my own
               bottle.

TOM   Come in, come in, and watch the feces hit the fan.

MALCOLM, *in a daze, automatically
               extends his hand.*

MALCOLM   Robert Ramsey. Welcome.

BOB   *(shaking* MALCOLM*'s hand)* Thank you. I
               thought if I gathered I might meet Miss Douglas.
               I've never met a woman with a past before.

TOM   That, lad, is highly unlikely. Get yourself a glass.

BOB *does so. Another customer,* EMMA
               DAY *or* BETH MacMILLAN *in disguise as
               "Dizzy Donohue," enters the store.*

MALCOLM   Robert, what's the man on the street saying?

BOB   They're calling it "The McTavish Purchase."

ANDY   "The McTavish Betrayal" is what it is! The nasty
               little bastard's upset the whole damned apple cart.

The back door swings open and SANDY
               roars in, in a fury.

SANDY
All right, where is he? I'll make mincemeat of him! *(shouting to* HOWARD, *in the Hardware)* Howard, where's David?

HOWARD
(in the doorway) They're over at Neilson's, looking at bridal wear.

SANDY
(on his way to his drink) I swear, I'll castrate the bugger by sundown! *(stopping in his tracks)* The kid's back! What is this? Initiation week? Didja bring your own bottle?

BOB
(showing it) I did, and I'm into it. *(gulps his drink)*

SANDY
(getting his drink) I heard the news, and I hied me out to see Lizzie Evans. For ten years that door opened and I was greeted with a hug. Well, the driver answered the door with the sourest mug you ever saw. Lizzie stood at the back of the hall with a hard look on her face. Hard, lads, hard as the whore's heart that's in her. She said terrible things about my sexual prowess, and worse about my egg-candling plant. Then she told me: three thousand dollars from the house painter, and she's off to grow mushrooms!

BOB
Mr. McTavish didn't do houses, he did interiors.

SANDY
I was in such a weakened condition, I upped the ante! I offered that little tart thirty-five hundred to stay in Raglan.

TOM
And what did Miss Evans reply?

SANDY
"Not bloody likely. I'm going to raise mushrooms all week," she says, "and buy a sailboat for the weekends. Excuse me, Sandy," she says, "I've got an appointment with a Samsonite suitcase." *(to* BOB*)* What's your name again?

MALCOLM
Robert Ramsey.

SANDY
Robert, I'm gonna tell you the difference between whores and wives.

BOB   I know that.

SANDY   It ain't sex—it's sympathy. I could bare my heart to Lizzie. I've got a bad elbow, y'know, from hockey years ago. Lizzie'd commiserate. "This, too, shall pass." Had a forger at the egg-candling plant, went on for a year. Andy caught him tracin' my signature at a window.

ANDY   *(proudly)* Wystan Llewelyn. Now behind bars.

SANDY   Lizzie'd commiserate. "This, too, shall pass." Bought bad stock on speculation, five-thousand do-re-mi's down the toilet, "This, too, shall pass."

TOM   Chisel the point, man, chisel the point!

SANDY   Tell all that to a wife, it don't ever pass. It goes on a list for future reference.

HOWARD *enters.*

HOWARD   S'cuse me. I've got an exchange. Fella bought lock washers when he needed flat.

ANDY, TOM, SANDY *and* MALCOLM *simultaneously droop their heads and groan:*

ALL   Dizzy Donohue.

HOWARD   *(resignedly)* Oh, yeah.

HOWARD *exits.* SANDY *sees* MALCOLM, *slumped in his chair, holding his head.*

SANDY   Malcolm? *(there is no reply)* Look at the old fossil. Turns into Jello when a wrench gets in the wheel.

MALCOLM   I'm contemplating strategy. You haven't heard the clincher. McTavish snuck into City Hall this morning and registered for Council!

Overlapping dialogue:

SANDY City Council??

TOM You don't say!

BOB Good for him!

ANDY Jumping Jesus!

SANDY It's a one-man insurrection!

"Dizzy Donohue" exits.

MALCOLM And he says to the clerk, in all his disarming innocence, "Please, sir, keep it mum." As if I don't know what goes on at City Hall! I know who changes the light bulbs, I know who waxes the floors. I know when the pigeons shit on the roof, and I hire the man who scrapes it off!

SANDY For Chrissake, Malcolm, he'll create chaos!

MALCOLM Lads, many before him have tried. Remember Artsy Arthur? *(explaining to* BOB*)* Wanted a sculptor to create a bronze thirty-foot wheat sheaf in front of City Hall. 'Member Greyhound Garth? Took the bus to Vermont one summer, came home wanting to cover all our damn bridges.

TOM But none before McTavish had a hundred and twenty grand.

MALCOLM *(rising, taking control)* And that's why the man's a powder keg! His brains have always been scrambled, but now he ain't wielding a brush, he's wielding a bloody fortune. So we have to contemplate strategy.

ANDY Strategy. How do we do that?

MALCOLM Andrew, strategy came to me with mother's milk. First, we don't have fisticuffs. *(to* SANDY*)* You don't castrate the bugger.

SANDY   But I'm left high and dry! I've got nothing on my
         horizon but a vacuum.

BOB   My science teacher said that nature always fills a
         vacuum.

SANDY   And that's what nature's conspiring to do! I've got
         Lizzie goin' west, and I've got Beth at home,
         wanting to adopt a bastard bairn!

MALCOLM Sandy, if McTavish gets on Council, he'll see all
         those tax rebates you get on the egg-candling plant.
         And, being McTavish, he will take umbrage.
         We've got to make the man an ally. So for once in
         your life, get your mind out of your crotch and
         hoist it up to your own self-interest. *(to* ANDY*)*
         And you, sir, will not even *hint* at Bolshevism.
         You'll make no accusations of betrayal. Because if
         McTavish gets on Council, he's going to wonder
         why all the town's bootleggers contribute so
         heavily to the Policemen's Benevolent Fund.

TOM   *When* he gets on Council. Money talks, and a
         hundred and twenty grand won't whisper, it'll
         bellow out to the populace.

MALCOLM It'll be absolutely deafening! So if we want
         McTavish in our camp, we'll listen to his plans.
         We'll see which way the wind's blowing, and we'll
         reconnoiter accordingly.

             HOWARD *turns off his lights, closing up.*

BOB   Like chameleons.

ANDY   Like what?

BOB   Chameleons change color according to their
         surroundings.

MALCOLM And that, laddie, is a valuable lesson from Darwin.
         Adaptation! Or, as my old dad used to say, "If
         you're brittle, you break— *(he claps his hands)* —if
         you're supple, you bend." *(he bends his wrists)*

SANDY   Are you sayin' we've got to put ethics aside and kiss the ass of the house painter?

MALCOLM   I'm sayin' bend your knees, pucker your lips, and queue up with the rest of the town.

TOM   Luckily, a hundred and twenty grand gives him plenty of surface.

> HOWARD *enters and gets a drink.*

HOWARD   David and Millie are comin' down the street. Sandy, I hear Lizzie's goin' west to corner the mushroom market.

SANDY   She is. And I hear your little drudge of a tenant wants elective office in Raglan.

HOWARD   It's a place to begin.

MALCOLM   Begin?

HOWARD   After that, there's always the country.

MALCOLM   *(in pain)* The country.

HOWARD   Yeah. "Mr. McTavish goes to Ottawa."

> DAVID *and* MILDRED *enter through the back door.*

DAVID   Say hello, gents, to Raglan's newest homeowners!

> *Overlapping dialogue:*

TOM   Howdy do!

MALCOLM   Greetings.

BOB   Mr. McTavish, I brought my own bottle.

DAVID   Good, Bob. I'm glad you're here.

MALCOLM   *(aside, to* SANDY *and* ANDY*)* Chameleons, lads,
                 chameleons!

ANDY   *(mustering strength)* David, I'd like to take this
                 opportunity to say congratulations on your
                 purchase. *(aside, to* SANDY*)* Sandy?

SANDY   Ditto, David. I say ditto.

DAVID   Thank you, Sandy.

MALCOLM   *(arm protruded)* Remember me, Millie? I'm
                 Malcolm MacGregor.

MILDRED   *(shaking hands)* I do.

HOWARD   Millie, this is our Police Chief, Andy Campbell.

ANDY   How do you do?

MILDRED   Hello.

HOWARD   Tom Wallace was manager of the bank—

MILDRED   I remember. Hello, Mr. Wallace.

TOM   I'm glad you've come home, Millie. This is young
                 Bob Ramsey from the King Eddie.

BOB   I'm pleased to make your acquaintance.

MILDRED   *(shaking his hand)* Aren't you the lad who brought
                 the cable?

BOB   I am.

                 The following is latently sexual. BOB
                 fondles MILDRED*'s hand throughout the
                 exchange.*

MILDRED   Are you one of the Ramseys from Spadina
                 Crescent?

BOB   I am.

MILDRED	Well, it must be in the genes. The Ramseys were always handsome people.
BOB	Thank you. Miss Douglas, I imagined you'd be a vision of loveliness, and you are.
MILDRED	Thank you, Bob. That's very flattering.
	SANDY *"removes"* BOB *from* MILDRED.
MALCOLM	David, we assumed you and Millie might buy a cottage for two with a picket fence. But we didn't know our man. And we didn't know our man harboured an ambition to sit on Council.
DAVID	I didn't think you'd know so soon.
BOB	He knows when the pigeons shit on the roof. *(to* MILDRED*)* Oh, Miss Douglas, forgive me. I ushally jis drink beer.
MILDRED	That's quite all right, Bob.
DAVID	Gentlemen, it's a splendid house. We'll have a housewarming, and we hope you'll all come help us christen it.
MALCOLM	It's admirable, David, absolutely admirable that you want to enter public service. You can rest assured that we, here in the gathering, pledge our support. *(he glares at* SANDY *and* ANDY*)*
SANDY	Full support.
ANDY	Laddie, you can count on it.
DAVID	Thank you.
MALCOLM	*(putting an arm around* DAVID*)* Now, David, in order to be effective on the Council, you'll have to navigate some murky waters. There's a veritable maze of personalities on the Council—not to mention a whole clutch of committees.

	Committees entrenched in the concrete of habit. I'm familiar with them all, because they reside on my turf, so to speak. If you'll let me take you under my wing, you won't have to run that gauntlet alone.
ANDY	What Malcolm's inferring, David, is you don't know your ass from your elbow so you'll need his guidance.
DAVID	Malcolm, I thank you for your offer, but I'll have to decline. Millie and I want to run an independent campaign with brand-new ideas.
MALCOLM	Independent?
DAVID	Yes.
MALCOLM	David, independence can be very prickly. What's paramount in all political endeavors is alignment.
DAVID	I agree completely. But I assumed, when you pledged your support, you'd be aligned behind my platform. You did pledge your support, didn't you?
SANDY	Full support.
ANDY	Laddie, you can count on it.
DAVID	Then you must be more than a little anxious to know what that platform will be. Millie and I have formulated a two-pronged plan. But before we begin, I'd like a drink.
MALCOLM	Certainly.
DAVID	*(going to the shelf)* Don't bother yourself, Malcolm, I'll get it myself. Mildred?
MILDRED	No, thank you.
DAVID	If you don't mind, I'd like my fiancé to begin.

> ANDY *mumbles "What?." SANDY
> mumbles "Beg your pardon?"*

DAVID   Would you, Mildred?

MILDRED   Gladly.

> *She takes center-stage. The men shuffle a
> bit, finding this untoward.*

At ease, gentlemen, at ease. Make yourselves comfortable. Now, you might find our first idea rather whimsical, but we want to do something that'll give us pleasure, as well as benefit the town. David and I love books. Our theme for David's campaign will be: *(with a flourish)* "Books on the Buses."

> *A pause. The men are incredulous.*

HOWARD   Sweet Petunia.

TOM   What was that?

SANDY   Books *where*?

ANDY   Books on the *buses*?

MILDRED   Yes. Fiction and poetry.

ANDY   Poetry? *(to* DAVID*)* You mean, like, "A always don't there B," on the buses?

DAVID   Malcolm, if the travelling public is large, and the reading public is small, why not kill two birds with one stone? Why not sneak a little literature into the hands of the registered voting public? At noon today I called the manufacturer of the new buses. I spoke to the president of the company.

MALCOLM   You actually spoke to Alistair Lundy?

DAVID   I did. In Oshawa. The news of the Sweepstakes went national, and he was more than gracious.

TOM	I said it first. Plenty of surface for all.
MILDRED	Mr. Lundy suggested that we remove two seats from the front of each bus. We'd put an aluminum rack in that space. David and I would donate the racks, and we'd pay for the labor involved.
DAVID	And we'd enlist Miss Logan's help in bulk purchasing.
MILDRED	You'd select a book when you entered the bus. You'd browse through it during your trip, and you'd be on your honour to return it to the rack when you reach your destination.
ANDY	They'll steal 'em, Mildred! They'll rob you blind!
MILDRED	We don't think they will. We think they'll monitor each other. We think they'll get hooked on something, they'll go to the library, seek that book out, take it home, and finish it. The net result is education and transportation rolled into one.
DAVID	I've tested this idea on the editor at the *Maple Leaf*. He said it was so original, it'd merit national coverage.
HOWARD	Malcolm, anything that's free is popular with the public. If you're smart, you'll hop onto David's bandwagon.
MALCOLM	David— *(downing his drink)* —I've hopped, and I'm seated.
DAVID	Thank you! Andy, where would the Police Department stand?
ANDY	*(downing his drink)* I'll have a word with my boys.
DAVID	Sandy, may I plaster my posters all 'round the egg-candling plant?
SANDY	You may.

DAVID	Fantastic. Now. *(with a new gravity)* Mildred and I have a second proposal, and it's considerably more substantial. Apparently there's a black-top highway going out Avenue A.
MALCOLM	How do you know that?
MILDRED	We've had an ear to a wall.
DAVID	We think *subsidized* housing should be built on the old Hogarth farm.
	The others are surprised. ANDY *mumbles "What?." * SANDY *mumbles "Land o' Goshen." * TOM *mumbles "What say?"*
MALCOLM	David, am I needin' a hearing aid, or did you say "subsidized" housing?
SANDY	No, no, no! Mildred, you got my words all garbled up. Malcolm, this is a problem of semitics. He means sub-divided housing.
MILDRED	No, we mean *subsidized* housing.
HOWARD	Holy Hollyhocks!
ANDY	Howard, if you persist with the flowers, I'm gonna vomit on your floor!
MILDRED	David and I would buy the farm and give it to the City. And we'd push the Council to develop it for lower-income people.
SANDY	*(sudden anger)* Sufferin' Succotash! Are you talking about rent-free housing?
BOB	*(in a sing-song)* If you're brittle, you break.
DAVID	Rent-supplemented housing.
SANDY	What the hell do you know about subsidized housing?

DAVID	I know that *your* dad gouged *my* dad for rent. If my dad had had a little help, I might have been sent to university.
SANDY	For God's sake, if they need to be subsidized, you'll get nothing but riff-raff.
DAVID	Sandy, you're such an expert on the devious, you can't get a grasp on the obvious. This isn't the British Isles—it's Canada. If you give decent, attractive housing to the under-class, their children'll graduate to the middle-class.
TOM	In the opinion of your elder statesman, it's a very advanced idea. It's shameful that some of our folk are huddling at night in the CN Station.
MALCOLM	David, subsidized housing's gonna be very, very delicate.
DAVID	I know that. *(smiling, and extending his hand to* MALCOLM*)* If you'll allow me, I'll slip under your wing on that one.
BOB	*(bouncing up on a box)* Mr. McTavish? *(all turn to the whoozy* BOB*)* May I say that it's a great privilege to be allowed to gather, here in this room. I've heard since I was a tad that all that transpires in Raglan begins in this room. I'm recently engaged, y'know, to Sally Abbott. She works in the China Department at Neilson's. Sells a lot of expensive Doulton figurines to Mrs. MacMillan. Sally and I earn minimum wage, a dollar an hour. I'd like to request that my name— *(to* SANDY*)* Robert Ramsey—be put on the list for subsidized housing. And I'd like to assure Mr. McTavish that we'll read his books on the bus ride out Avenue A.
DAVID	When there's a list, Bobby, you'll be at the top.
BOB	Thank you, sir, you've just got two votes. *(he sits)*

DAVID   Malcolm, you've always said a Councilman has to
                     be married. We've set Saturday, the 20th, and
                     you're all invited. We'll live in the grandest house
                     in town, which I hope will become a hub of
                     progressive political activity.

                              There is a knock at the back door. BETH
                              MacMILLAN enters, lugging a large, heavy
                              picnic basket.

BETH   May I come in?

MILDRED   Why, Beth, good evening.

DAVID   Hello, Beth.

                              The others, uncertain of BETH's purpose,
                              are embarrassed. They shift positions,
                              waiting.

BETH   Hello, Sandy.

SANDY   Hello, Beth.

MILDRED   Did you come to fetch your husband?

BETH   *(moving to SANDY)* No, I came to join him.
                     Sandy and I had lunch together today and I thought,
                     well, lunch *and* dinner would make it a red-letter
                     day.

                              The others move away slightly, giving them
                              space for "privacy."

SANDY   You've heard bout the McTavish purchase?

BETH   I have. *(compassionately)* Sandy, this, too, shall
                     pass.

SANDY   Thank you, Beth. That's very nice of you.

BETH   *(privately, to SANDY)* In the meantime, there's
                     going to be a wedding.

SANDY	Yes, there is.
BETH	We'll attend, and listen to those hard, uphill vows once again.
SANDY	We will. What's that you're lugging?
BETH	I've made a casserole for the gathering. It's your favorite dish. Finnan Haddie.
SANDY	Didja use real cream, or tinned Carnation?
BETH	I went the whole hog, Sandy. Real cream.
MILDRED	Beth, this is Bob Ramsey, from the King Eddie telegraph.
BETH	How do you do?
BOB	*(quite drunk)* Mrs. MacMillan, I've had my ear to a wall.
BETH	Oh?
BOB	*(leaning in to her)* Forty percent off Doulton figurines at Neilson's next Monday.
BETH	Really? Thank you for telling me. I'll be the first in line, at nine. Now, let's have the Haddie.
MILDRED	There's such a crowd of us, Beth.
BETH	I've made plenty. *(opening the basket)* And I brought salad, and plates, and forks. I know the distaff side has always been excluded from the gathering, but I assumed Millie'd be here, and I thought, well, Heavens, it is dinnertime, and they do all have to eat. *(pause; she falters)* And I recalled what Genesis said in the olive grove: *(to SANDY)* "The woman thou gavest to be with me, gave me of the tree, and I did eat." Well. I've got pickles, and aspic—

MILDRED   Let me help you lay it out.

BETH   Let's do a buffet, on that table.

> *Two men move* DAVID*'s table.*

TOM   Beth, will it keep a minute?

BETH   Certainly.

TOM   I'd like, if I may, to speak personally for a moment.

> *Ad libs as they gather around* TOM*: "Of course, Tom," "Go ahead," "By all means," "Certainly."*

TOM   *(refilling his glass)* The years fly by, and the joints seize up, and you're left with a medicine chest full of prescriptions. And you know more people under the ground than above it. *(he takes center-stage)* I've felt, much of my life, that I've been in a boxing ring with God. He spars, and jabs, and every now and then he packs a helluva wallop. '14 to '18 I lost a brother at Vimy Ridge. Came home in a coffin, without legs. In the dirty Thirties I lost my father's farm. Dieppe took my only son. Two weeks ago, reflecting on all this, I concluded I'd had enough. I knelt by my bed and asked the Almighty to take me.

Today, when I look around the room, I see this twig over here. Bob Ramsey's only just getting a leg-up on the ladder. David and Millie are just now getting a foothold. Malcolm and Andy have to do some financial retrenching at City Hall. Howard's losing his tenant, but gaining, hopefully, a voice on the Council for himself and sister Jane. Sandy and Beth have the hardest job of all. Forgiving.

But you're all on the brink of new departures. And so am I—by extension—and I thank you for it. Today, I want at least another year! I want to dance with Millie at her wedding. I want to lick envelopes for David's campaign. And if you win, David, I'll help you fill the book racks on the buses. And I am, I tell you, *chomping at the bit* to see McTavish babies runnin' around the whorehouse. This is a matter of some urgency, David, so I hope you'll set about it without delay. Enough said. Time to eat, drink, and be merry.

3

> *There is a flurry of activity.* BETH *lifts a tablecloth into the air.*
>
> *As the lights begin to dim, we hear ad libs: "Malcolm, move the trundle." "Howard, get more glasses." "Bobby, clear that surface." "Sandy, lift that carton."*
>
> *In the midst of this activity, the lights fade and we see* DAVID *and* MILDRED *kiss under a pin-spot.*
>
> *Music up. Suggested music: "(The Bells are Ringing) For Me and My Gal."*
>
> *Curtain.*

Dec 21/07

Cast in the Blyth Festival Production

Emma   *Sharon Bakker*
Andy   *Eric Coates*
Sandy   *Ari Cohen*
Beth   *Michelle Fisk*
Tom   *Jerry Franken*
Malcolm   *Thomas Hauff*
Howard   *Michael Healey*
David   *Ross Manson*
Bob   *Jason Rumley*
Mildred   *Jane Spidell*

Directed by Paul Lampert
Set and Costume Design by Yvonne Sauriol
Lighting Design by Bonnie Beecher
Assistant Director, Eric Coates
Production Stage Manager, Michael Wallace
Assistant Stage Manager, Christine Oakey